KINGDOM BIBLE STUDY
PROGRAM FOR SUNDAY SCHOOLS

Laying the Right Foundation for a Future Generation

11-12 Years

Abraham John

Genesis Project 126

BIBLE STUDY PROGRAM FOR SUNDAY SCHOOL CHILDREN (AGES 11-12 YEARS OLD)

Copyright © 2025 Abraham John

Published by Tree of Life
For The Kingdom University

www.TheKingdomUniversity.org
email: admin@TheKingdomUniversity.org
1(800) 558 5020

ISBN: 978-1-948330-53-4

Printed in the United States of America

All emphasis or additions within Scripture quotations are the author's own.

Unless otherwise indicated, all Scripture quotations are taken from the New King James Version of the Holy Bible. Copyright ©1995-2010, The Zondervan Corporation. All Rights Reserved.

Scripture quotations marked CEV are taken from the Contemporary English Version (Bible for Today's Family). Copyright ©American Bible Society 1991, 1992, 1995; Anglicizations British and Foreign Bible; Society 1996. All rights reserved.

Scripture quotations marked ESV® are from The Holy Bible, English Standard Version® (ESV®) ©2001 by Crossway, a publishing ministry of Good News Publishers. All rights reserved.

Scripture quotations are taken from the Amplified Bible® (AMPC®) © 1954, 1958, 1962, 1964, 1965, 1987 by The Lockman Foundation. Used by permission lockman.org

All rights reserved. No part of this book may be reproduced or transmitted in any form or by any means, electronic or mechanical—including photocopying, recording, or by any information storage and retrieval system without permission in writing from the author.

Please direct your inquiries to admin@TheKingdomUniversity.org

TABLE OF CONTENTS

Introduction to Bible Study	7
BOOK 2: CHILDREN 11-12 YEARS OLD	**11**
PART 1: WHO AM I?	**13**
Lesson 1: I Am A Spirit Living In A Body	15
Lesson 2: I Am A Child Of God	19
Lesson 3: I Will Live Forever	15
Lesson 4: I Am A Male-Child, And I Am Created In The Very Likeness And Image Of God	19
Lesson 5: I Am A Female-Child	33
Lesson 6: I Am Just Like My Heavenly Father	37
Lesson 7: Function Like My Heavenly Father	41
Lesson 8: I Can Imagine	45
Lesson 9: I Am A King	49
Lesson 10: I Am A Queen	53
Lesson 11: I Am Creative Like My Father	57
Lesson 12: I Am Being Trained: To Become A Man, A Husband, And A Father	61
Lesson 13: I Am Being Trained To: Become A Woman, A Wife, And A Mother	65
Lesson 14: I Am Created To Bring Life And Be Productive	69
Lesson 15: I Am Created To Conceive And Give Birth To God's Purpose On The Earth	73
Lesson 16: I Am Beautiful In Spirit, In Soul, And In Body	77
Lesson 17: I Am An Original	81
Lesson 18: I Speak Like My Heavenly Father	84
Lesson 19: I Am Loved By My Heavenly Father	88

TABLE OF CONTENTS

PART 2: WHY AM I HERE? — 93

Lesson 20: I Am Created In God's Image And Likeness — 95
Lesson 21: I Am Created To Have Dominion — 98
Lesson 22: My Purpose Is Connected To The Earth — 101
Lesson 23: I Am A Manager And An Influencer — 104
Lesson 24: I Am A Builder And A Repairer — 107
Lesson 25: I Am Called To Lead — 110
Lesson 26: I Can Subdue And Overcome — 113
Lesson 27: I Am Called To Excel And Grow — 116
Lesson 28: I Can Be Productive And Fruitful — 119
Lesson 29: I Am Here To Establish And Restore — 122
Lesson 30: I Have Gifts And Talents — 128
Lesson 31: I Am A Problem Solver — 131
Lesson 32: I Am Fearless — 134
Lesson 33: I Am Part Of A Bigger Picture — 137
Lesson 34: I Make A Difference — 140
Lesson 35: I Need Wisdom And Help — 143
Lesson 36: I Am A Blessing — 146
Lesson 37: I Protect And Care — 148
Lesson 38: I Rebuild Relationships — 150
Lesson 39: I Am Created To Rule In My Area — 153
Lesson 40: I Represent God's Kingdom — 158
Lesson 41: Creation Is Waiting For Me — 161

PART 3: WHERE DID I COME FROM? — 165

Lesson 42: I Come From God — 167
Lesson 43: I Come From Heaven — 170

TABLE OF CONTENTS

Lesson 44: I Come From The Kingdom Of Heaven	173
Lesson 45: I Am A Kingdom Ambassador	176
Lesson 46: I Am Designed By God Almighty	179
Lesson 47: I Am Skilfully And Wonderfully Made	182
Lesson 48: I Need The Kingdom Of God	185
Lesson 49: God Sent Me To Do His Work	188
Lesson 50: Nobody Else Can Do What I Do	192
Lesson 51: God Needs Me On This Earth	195
Lesson 52: The Earth Is My Permanent Home	198

MORE BOOKS AND RESOURCES   **203**

INTRODUCTION TO THE BIBLE STUDY PROGRAM

Train up a child in the way he should go, and when he is old he will not depart from it (Proverbs 22:6).

The Tree of Life children's Bible Study Program is thoughtfully designed to lay a firm spiritual foundation in the hearts and minds of young children during their most formative years.

Rooted in the principles of Kingdom Education, this program aims to help children discover their identity, understand their purpose, and know their origin.

At the core of the program are three foundational books authored by Dr. Abraham John. These include the following:

1. Who Am I?
2. Why Am I Here?
3. Where Did I Come From?

Knowing that every human being will ask these questions and the importance of it, God Almighty answered all of them in the very first chapter of the Bible. As I share in my books and teachings, Genesis 1:26 is the **purpose statement** for mankind, given by our Creator. We've neglected it, thinking it's just an Old Testament creation story.

Your spirit came into this world fully aware and with the knowledge of who you are and why you were sent to this earth. Instead of welcoming and nurturing that spirit to release what they were sent here for, most children are trained in the ways of this world. The environment in which we were born and raised plays a role in brainwashing and forming a wrong mindset in us.

INTRODUCTION TO THE BIBLE STUDY PROGRAM

To be born a male or a female is a natural process, but becoming a man or woman is intentional, just like no one becomes a pilot, a doctor, or a scientist by birth. They have to go through intense training to become that.

The lessons are directed to both boys and girls independently of the topic, because both genders need to understand the respective role of each other in order to live in harmony with one another and fulfill their God given purpose.

The curriculum is designed as a repeating annual cycle, allowing students to revisit these vital themes each year. This repetition deepens their understanding as they grow and mature, preparing them to carry a clear sense of identity, purpose, and divine origin, as they transition through each stage of their development.

Four Key Kingdom Educational Stages

This complete program is aligned with four key educational stages in the Kingdom framework, being the following:

- **Kindergarten Stage (Ages 0 to 5 years old)**: These early years focus on laying a strong foundation for their identity, purpose, and origin. Through engaging visuals, brief thematic introductions, and songs, young children begin to explore fundamental questions such as Who am I?, Why am I here?, and Where did I come from?. They are divided into two groups in order to address their respective developmental needs:

  » Infants and Toddlers (0 to 2 years old), and
  » Preschoolers (3 to 5 years old).

INTRODUCTION TO THE BIBLE STUDY PROGRAM

- **Primary Level (Ages 6 to 12 years old)**

  » Lower Primary (6 to 8 years old) : At this stage, children build upon the foundation laid in preschool, deepening their understanding of identity, calling, and life purpose. This is achieved through the use of the original three-book set, along with accompanying coloring books that reinforce key themes in an engaging and age-appropriate way.

  » Upper Primary (9 to 12 years old) : At this stage, children strengthen the foundation laid in earlier years and begin to explore their unique gifts, strengths, and calling. They are encouraged to identify their personal strengths and understand how these relate to their life's purpose, helping them form a clearer sense of direction and identity.

- **Secondary Level (Ages 13 to 17)**: This phase focuses on training and development, equipping senior school scholars to nurture their talents and prepare for a life of excellence ahead. The goal is to help them hone their gifts in anticipation of fulfilling their respective callings. These youthful scholars are divided into two age groups:

  » Lower Secondary (12 to 14 years old) and
  » Upper Secondary (15 to 17 years old).

- **College and University Level (Ages 18-plus)**: With a solid foundation in their identity and purpose, students at the university level are empowered to apply their learning in real-world contexts. Through mentoring and coaching, they are supported as they exercise dominion in their specific areas of calling; ultimately becoming leaders and agents of transformation in their respective fields of further study and endeavor.

The Tree of Life children's Bible Study Program is a spiritual journey designed to raise confident, purpose-driven young adults who know who they are, why they're here, and where they come from; and who are later sent out to fulfill their Divine purpose and callings in life.

Abraham John
Tree of Life

BOOK 2

Children 11-12 Years old

LESSON 1: I AM A SPIRIT LIVING IN A BODY

Learning Objectives:

By the end of this lesson, children will be able to:

1. Recognize that humans are both physical and spiritual beings, with the spirit giving life to their bodies, as shown in the Bible (Genesis 2:7, John 6:63, 1 Corinthians 6:19).

2. Acknowledge that their bodies are the temple of the Holy Spirit; and, that God dwelling within gives them purpose, power and meaning to their existence.

3. Appreciate the special nature of their lives, understanding that they are more than just physical bodies; they are living beings with a spirit, created by God, and dwelling with His presence.

4. Think about their own spiritual identity, and what it means to have the Holy Spirit living inside of them, and how this affects their daily lives.

Story: The Clay Man

Prince was a curious boy who loved learning how things were made. One afternoon, he watched a movie about the creation — and his eyes lit up with wonder! He saw how God made the very first man from the dust of the ground.

"Wait—did God really make a person out of dirt?" Prince asked, running to his mom.

"Yes, He did, because our Purpose is connected to the Earth" she said with a smile. She opened her Bible and pointed to Genesis 2:7 (NKJV): **"And the Lord God formed man of the dust of the ground, and breathed into his nostrils the breath of life; and man became a living being."**

Prince's jaw dropped. "That's amazing!" Right away, he ran to get some clay. He rolled it, and then shaped it into a little person—with a head, arms, legs, and even tiny feet. Then, he leaned in close, took a big breath, and blew on it.
But nothing happened. The little clay man just sat there, not moving at all. Prince looked confused. "Why didn't it come to life?"

His mom knelt down beside him. "Because only God can give life," she said gently. "The Bible says in John 6:63 (NKJV): **"It is the Spirit who gives life; the flesh profits nothing"** "and, 1 Corinthians 6:19 says, **"Do you not know that your body is the temple of the Holy Spirit who is in you, whom you have from God?"**

Prince's eyes lit up. "So... my body is like a house for the Holy Spirit?"

"Exactly," said his mom. "That's why your life is so special—God gave it to you, and He lives in you when you believe in Him."

Prince smiled and held up his little clay man. "You may not be alive," he whispered to it, "but I am—and God lives in me!

Questions:

1. What did God use to make the first man?
2. What did Prince do after watching the movie about the creation?
3. Why didn't Prince's clay man come to life?
4. What does John 6:63 say gives true life?
5. Where does the Holy Spirit lives if you believe in Jesus?
6. What does it mean to you that the Holy Spirit lives inside you?

Memory Verse

Genesis 2:7 "And the Lord God formed man of the dust of the ground, and breathed into his nostrils the breath of life; and man became a living being." (NKJV)

Activity: Mirror Game

Practical Activity:

Mirror Game Instructions:

1. Kids look in a mirror, and say what they see.
2. Then ask, "Can you see your kindness, or your love, or your thoughts?"
3. Explain that our spirit can't be seen but is still real.

Notes:

LESSON 2: I AM A CHILD OF GOD

Learning Objectives:

By the end of this lesson, children will be able to:

1. Understand that, through faith in Jesus Christ, they are adopted into God's family and have the privilege of being called His children (John 1:12, Romans 8:14-15).

2. Realize that God's love is unwavering, always welcoming, and never depends on their behavior or actions; unlike the conditional love, as seen in some animal kingdoms or some human relationships (Romans 5:8).

3. Appreciate that through Christ's sacrifice, they have been accepted into a family where God's love is constant, even when they make mistakes, and where they can always rely on His care and His protection.

4. Think about what it means by being a child of God, to develop a deeper sense of safety, belonging, and thankfulness toward God for His loving, selfless actions (Romans 5:8).

Story: God's Family

John loved watching animal shows. He liked learning about how different animals live, and how they take care of their families.

One day, he watched a show about lions. It was very exciting—until something sad happened. A young lion cub tried to eat before the father lion, and so the father growled, and chased the cub away.

The little lion cub had to leave and find food on his own.

John felt upset. "That's so unfair," he thought. "What if parents did that to their children?"

Later that night, John picked up his Bible. As he read, he remembered something really special.

"Wait a minute," he said. "God's love isn't like the lions!"
He remembered a Bible verse that he had learnt: John 1:12—
"But to all who believed him and accepted him, he gave the right to become children of God."

And another verse popped into his head:
Romans 8:14-15 **"Those who are led by the Spirit of God are God's children. You didn't receive a spirit that makes you afraid. Instead, you received the Spirit of adoption. That's why we call God, our 'Abba, Father!'"**

John's eyes lit up. "That means God chose me to be part of His family! I'm His child!"

He ran to tell his mom. "Mom! I'm God's child! And He never sends His children away, even if they mess up, right?"

"That's right," she said with a smile. "God's love doesn't work like the lion family. In God's family, His love never runs out."

She added, Romans 5:8 says **"But God demonstrates His own love toward us, in that while we were still sinners, Christ died for us."**

That shows how much God loves us."

John thought about the lion pack's family again. In their animal kingdom, the father eats first, and the others have to wait. But in God's Kingdom, it's the other way around. Jesus, the King, gave up His own life so we could be part of God's family.

John looked up at the sky and whispered, "Thank You, Abba. Thank You for always loving me."

Memory Verse

John 1:12—"But to all who believed him and accepted him, he gave the right to become children of God."

Activity: Role Play – Welcome to the Kingdom Family!

The Characters (6 to 8 actors):

- **Narrator**: can be a teacher or student
- **Peter** – a student, who's feeling lost and unimportant
- **John** – a friend, who knows about God's love
- **Mr. Leonel** – a Sunday School teacher
- **Martha** a –girl, who feels like she needs to "earn" love
- **Paul** –another boy, who acts out, because he doesn't think he's loved by anyone
- **Voice** – represents God's voice of truth (can also be played as a voiceover or spotlight moment)
- **Extra children** (if needed) – classmates, as background characters

Scene 1: The Schoolyard

- **Story-teller**: It's Monday morning. Peter sits alone on the bench at recess/school-break, watching the other kids laugh and play. But something inside Peter feels empty.
- **Peter**: (Sighs) I don't get it. I try to fit in, I try to do the right thing… but it still feels like I don't matter to anyone.
- **John**: (Sits next to Peter) Hey, you okay?
- **Peter**: Not really. Do you ever feel like you have to be perfect for people to like you?
- **John**: Yeah, I used to think that. But then I learnt something that totally changed the way I see myself.
- **Peter**: What's that?
- **John**: That I'm a child of God. Like, not just a believer—but a part of His family. He chose me, even when I mess up.
- **Peter**: Wait, seriously? Even when you're not perfect?
- **John**: Especially then! That's what makes His love so different. It doesn't depend on what we do. (Romans 5:8)

Scene 2: Sunday School Classroom

- **Mr. Leonel**: Okay class, today we're learning about being children of God. Can anyone tell me what adoption means?
- **Martha**: Isn't that when someone gets chosen to be part of a family, even if they weren't born into it?
- **Mr. Leonel**: Exactly! And guess what? When we believe in Jesus, we're adopted into God's family. We're His children! (John 1:12)
- **Paul**: (Pouting) But why would God want someone like me? I mess up all the time.

- **Mr. Leonel**: That's the amazing part, Paul. God doesn't love us because we're perfectly good. He loves us because He is love. He sent Jesus for us while we were still sinners. (Romans 5:8)
- **John (to class)**: It's like we're all invited into the greatest family ever. We don't have to earn it—rather, it's a gift.

Scene 3: A Moment of Reflection

- **Story-teller**: Later that night, Peter sits on the bed. He's thinking about what John and Mr. Leonel said earlier.
- **Peter**: (Talking to himself) So… I really am a child of God? He adopted me? And He Loves me even when I mess up?
- **Voice**: Yes, Peter. You are Mine. You belong to me. You are loved not because of what you do, but because of Who I Am.
- **Peter**: (Smiles) I don't have to be perfect… I just have to be His. Thank You, God.

Scene 4: Back at School

- **Story-teller**: The next day, Peter walks into school with a smile on his whole face. Something has changed inside him.
- **Martha**: Hey Peter, you seem happier today.
- **Peter**: I just realized… I'm part of God's family. No matter what happens, I'm loved by Him. And, that means, I can love other people too.
- **Paul**: (Smiles) That's pretty cool. Maybe I want to be part of that family too.
- **John**: You already are—if you believe in Jesus, you're in!

Closing Story

- **Story-teller**: God's love is unconditional, and being His child, means you are always welcomed, always wanted, and always protected. No matter your past, your mistakes, or your doubts— you are a child of God.

To Ponder:

Ask the class:

- What does it mean to you personally to be a child of God?
- How does knowing you are adopted into God's family change the way you see yourself and other people?

Notes:

LESSON 3: I WILL LIVE FOREVER

Learning Objectives:

By the end of this lesson, children will be able to:

1. Recognize that through Jesus' death and His resurrection, believers are promised everlasting life with God (John 11:25-26, Revelation 21:3-4).

2. Understand that Jesus' victory over death means that death is not the end for believers, and they can live forever with God in His presence, free from pain and sorrow.

3. Reflect on the joy of eternal life, understanding it as a source of hope and comfort for the present and the future.

Story: Osvaldo's Joyful Night

One quiet evening, Osvaldo sat beside his mom as she read to him from the Bible about Jesus' death on the cross. As she described how Jesus was hurt and died, Osvaldo's eyes filled with tears.

"Why did Jesus have to suffer so much?" he asked softly.

His mom gently hugged him. "It's okay to feel sad, Osvaldo. Jesus went through all of that because He loves us so much. But, guess what?" she said with a smile. "That's not the end of the story!"

She opened the Bible again, and read from John 11:25-26 (NKJV): **"Jesus said, 'I am the resurrection and the life. He who believes in Me, though he may die, he shall live. And whoever lives and believes in Me shall never die.'"**

Osvaldo's eyes lit up. "So... Jesus came back to life?"

"That's right!" his mom said. "Jesus didn't stay in the grave. He arose again, and because of Him, we don't have to be afraid of death. We'll live forever with God!"

Osvaldo's heart felt light and full of hope. He smiled big, and asked, "What will it be like when we live with God?"

His mom turned to the last book in the Bible, and read from Revelation 21:3-4(NKJV): **"Behold, the tabernacle of God is with men, and He will dwell with them... God shall wipe away all tears from their eyes; and there shall be no more death, neither sorrow, nor crying, neither shall there be any more pain."**

"Wow," Osvaldo whispered. "That sounds like the happiest place ever."

"It is," his mom said. "And because of Jesus, we get to be there forever."

That night, Osvaldo lay in bed with a big smile on his face. He wasn't sad anymore. He felt peaceful and excited, knowing that Jesus was alive—and that one day, he would live forever with Him.

Questions:

1. Why did Osvaldo feel sad when his mom read about Jesus dying on the cross?
2. What did Jesus say to Martha in John 11:25-26?
3. Why is Jesus coming back to life, so important?
4. How did Osvaldo feel after learning Jesus is alive?
5. What does Revelation 21:3-4 tell us about living with God one day?
6. What are you most excited about when you think about living forever with God?

Memory Verse

John 11:25 "Jesus said to her, 'I am the resurrection and the life. He who believes in Me, though he may die, he shall live.'" (NKJV)

Activity: "Forever with Jesus"

What you need: Paper and Crayons or colored markers

What to do:

1. Draw a picture of a happy home with Jesus.
2. Talk about how Jesus loves you, and how He wants you to live forever with Him.
3. Share your drawing with your family or friends, and tell them about Jesus's promise of life forever!

Notes:

LESSON 4: I AM A MALE-CHILD, AND I AM CREATED IN THE VERY LIKENESS AND IMAGE OF GOD

Learning Objectives:

By the end of this lesson, children will be able to:

1. Recognize that they have a unique identity and purpose that reflects God's character and creativity (Genesis 1:26).

2. Understand that being made in God's image, calls them to reflect His qualities, such as His wisdom, His love, and His justice; and to live in such a way that honors Him, by fulfilling their roles in life with integrity and care.

3. Learn from God's example and imitate Him as Jesus imitated the Father and taught us to do the same (John 5:19).

4. Understand that being made in God's image, empowers them with imagination beyond measure.

5. Develop an understanding of what it means to be a male-child created in God's image, including their unique roles, responsibilities, and the example they should set for others, showing godly leadership and godly wisdom.

Story: A Role Model

In a mighty kingdom, there lived a wise and kind king. One bright morning, he called his young son, the prince. "Come with me," he said. "There's something important I want to show you."

They rode through the kingdom together—past fields, rivers, and busy villages full of people. Everywhere they went, the prince saw farmers working, children playing, and kingdom guards protecting the towns.

"One day," the king said gently, "all of this will be yours. But remember—being a king isn't just about wearing a crown or having riches. It's about leading with wisdom and protecting those who depend on you."

The prince looked around, thoughtfully. "I never thought of it like that," he said. "I want to be a good king like you, Father."

The king smiled. "Then watch me, learn from me, and follow what is right. That's what makes a true leader." That evening, the prince remembered something his teacher had told him from the Bible: Genesis 1:26 – ***"So God created man in His own image and likeness."***

His likeness, means we are to function like God; and image means imagination, because when God wants something, He first imagine it.. and we were created to be like Him.

Then he remembered what Jesus said in John 5:19 (NKJV): **"The Son can do nothing of Himself, but what He sees the Father do; for whatever He does, the Son also does in like manner."**

From that day on, The Prince worked hard to learn more about God—so that one day, he could rule not just with power, but in the likeness and Image of God.

Questions:

1. Where did the king take his son, the prince?
2. What lesson did the king want the prince to learn?
3. Why is it important to have good role models?
4. Who are some people in your life that you can learn from and follow as role models?

Memory Verse

John 5:19 "The Son can do nothing of Himself, but what He sees the Father do; for whatever He does, the Son also does in like manner."(NKJV)

Practical Activity: The Royal Obstacle Course Run

Instructions:

1. Set up a fun mini obstacle course
2. where, boys:
- ★ carry a toy sword

- ★ rescue a stuffed animal, and
- ★ "protect" a village (pile of blocks).
3. The goal? Teach them that real strength is about protecting others, not just being strong.

Notes:

LESSON 5: I AM A FEMALE-CHILD

Learning Objectives:

By the end of this lesson, children will be able to:

1. Recognize that, just like men, women are created in God's image, with equal value, purpose, and dignity (Genesis 1:27). God created women to be partners in His plan, reflecting His beauty, grace, and strength.

2. Understand that while men and women have different roles, they are equally valued by God; and are meant to work together in harmony, reflecting the unity and partnership God intended from the beginning (Genesis 2:18-24).

3. Develop an appreciation for their identity as female children created by God, understanding their real worth and special purpose in His kingdom.

4. Learn the beauty of mutual respect and cooperation, recognizing that they, as female children, are designed to walk beside others, contributing to a world of love, harmony, and unity as God intended.

Story: Someone Special

Long ago, the great and loving King created a wonderful world full of bright stars, tall trees, and deep oceans.

Then, He made a very special son to care for it all. The King shaped the man from the dust of the ground, and the man came to life with the King's own breath.

But the King saw that something was missing.

The man was strong and wise, but he was alone. So the King said, "It is not good for the man to be alone. I will make a helper, who is just right for him."

The King gently caused the man to fall into a deep sleep. Then, He took out one of the man's ribs, and used it to create someone very special—a woman.

She was not made from his head to rule over him, nor from his feet to be beneath him, but from his side—to walk beside him. She was made with beauty, grace, and strength, to be his partner in love and unity.

The man woke up, saw her, and said with joy, "This is now bone of my bones, and flesh of my flesh!"

The King smiled, because His plan was perfect.

The Bible says in Genesis 1:27(NKJV), **"So God created man in His own image; in the image of God He created him; male and female He created them."**

Both the man and the woman were created in God's image, with different roles but equal value. The King made them to work together—each one special, each one loved.

From that day forward, they walked together, side by side, caring for the world and each other, just as the King intended.

Questions:

1. Why did the King decide to make a woman?
2. How did the King create the woman?
3. What does it mean that the woman was made from the man's side?
4. What does Genesis 1:27 teach us about people?
5. How were the man and woman meant to live and work together?

Memory Verse

Genesis 1:27 "So God created man in His own image; in the image of God He created him; male and female He created them." (NKJV)

Practical Activity: Heart and Rib Puzzle Craft

Instructions:

1. Give each girl a heart-shaped piece of paper, and cut it into two pieces.
2. One side represents the man and the other the woman.
3. When put together, it forms a complete heart, showing how God made them to work together.

Notes:

LESSON 6: I AM JUST LIKE MY HEAVENLY FATHER

Learning Objectives:

By the end of this lesson, children will be able to:

1. Understand that, as God's children, they are made to reflect His character and nature, just like a child imitates their parents (Ephesians 5:1, John 5:19).

2. Recognize that God's nature is full of His mercy, His kindness, His patience, and His truth; and that they are called to reflect these qualities in their own lives (Exodus 34:6).

3. Grasp the idea that by observing and following Jesus' example, they can live a life that mirrors God's love and goodness; by treating others with the same grace and compassion that He shows (John 5:19).

4. Recognize that every kind action, forgiving word, or thoughtful gesture is a way to show the world a little picture of God's heart and His character.

5. Cultivate an attitude of joy in imitating God, realizing that by reflecting His love in daily life, they become more like their Heavenly Father.

Story: A photocopy

One exciting day, our family got a new dog—a friendly, gentle female dog to be a companion for our male dog. They became best friends, and before long, they had a puppy together!

When the puppy was born, we were all so surprised—it looked just like its father! As it grew, we noticed even more: it walked like him, it played like him, and it even tilted its head the same funny way. We couldn't help but laugh. It was like looking at a little copy of the dad!

Watching them, made me think about something very special: we're kind of like that puppy.

The Bible tells us that we were made to reflect our Heavenly Father. In Ephesians 5:1(NKJV), it says, **"Therefore be imitators of God as dear children."**

Just like children often copy their parents, we are called to follow God—learning to love, to forgive, and to care like He does. Even Jesus, God's own Son, said something amazing in John 5:19(NKJV): **"The Son can do nothing of Himself, but what He sees the Father do; for whatever He does, the Son also does in like manner."**

Jesus showed us how to live by watching and obeying His Father—and we can do the same! And what is our Father like?

The Bible tells us in Exodus 34:6(NKJV), **"God is merciful and gracious, slow to anger, and abounding in goodness and truth."** That is the kind of life we are meant to live—full of God's mercy, His kindness, His patience, and His truth.

So just like the little puppy follows its father, we can follow our Heavenly Father, by showing His love in everything we do. And every time we do something kind, forgiving, or creative, we are showing the world a little picture of the Father.

Discussion Questions:

1. What surprised the family about the new puppy?
2. How are we like that little puppy?
3. What does Ephesians 5:1 tell us to do?
4. How did Jesus show us how to live?
5. What are some things God is like, according to Exodus 34:6?
6. What are some ways we can imitate our Heavenly Father?
7. Can you think of a time when you acted like God—by showing love or kindness?

Memory Verse

Ephesians 5:1 "Therefore be imitators of God as dear children."(NKJV)

Activity: Kind Words & Hurtful Words Sorting Game

1. Write words on paper strips, such as "You are special!" and "I don't like you!"
2. Kids sort these into two baskets—one labeled "Like God," and another labeled "Not Like God."

Notes:

LESSON 7: FUNCTION LIKE MY HEAVENLY FATHER

Learning Objectives:

By the end of this lesson, children will be able to:

1. Recognize that through God's promises, they can participate in His divine nature, reflecting His qualities such as love, kindness, patience, and mercy in their daily actions (2 Peter 1:3-4).

2. Understand that, just as God shows kindness and mercy to them even when they fall short, they are called to respond with similar grace to others, even in challenging circumstances (Micah 6:8).

3. Learn that acting justly, loving mercy, and walking humbly with God are ways they can mirror God's character in their relationships with others (Micah 6:8).

4. Understand that when they reflect God's kindness and love, it can positively influence those around them, helping others to see a glimpse of God's love through their behavior.

5. Be inspired to follow Paul's example, by choosing to act with mercy, patience, and humility, showing God's love in both easy and difficult situations.

Story: Paul's Big Heart

Paul was a boy with a big heart—he was gentle, kind, and always ready to help. But not everyone treated him the same way. Some kids at school teased him and tried to make him upset.

But Paul didn't yell, fight, or try to get back at them. Instead, he stayed calm. He smiled, helped others when they needed it, and even shared his snack with one of the boys who had been mean to him the day before.

One of his friends asked, "Why are you still nice to them?" Paul thought for a while and said, "Because God is kind to me, even when I mess up. I want to be like Him."

Paul's kindness wasn't just about being a good kid—it was a reflection of God's heart.

The Bible says in 2 Peter 1:3-4 that God has given us His great promises so that we can be partakers of His divine nature.

That means, when we follow God, we can live like Him—showing His love, His patience, and His mercy, just like He does.

Another verse Paul had learned in Sunday school was from Micah 6:8: **"He has shown you, O man, what is good; and what does the Lord require of you? To act justly, to love mercy, and to walk humbly with your God."**

Paul knew that loving mercy meant forgiving others and being kind, even when it wasn't easy. And that is exactly what he chose to do.

Because of his gentle spirit, some of the kids who once teased Paul started to change.

They began to see something different in him—something peaceful, something strong. They were seeing a little picture of God's love through Paul. And that is what made Paul's heart so big—it was filled with God's kindness, and he shared it with everyone around him.

Questions:

1. How did Paul treat the kids who were mean to him?
2. Why did Paul choose to be kind even when it was hard?
3. What does it mean to be a "partaker of God's divine nature"?
4. What does Micah 6:8 say God wants us to do?
5. What is mercy, and how did Paul show it?
6. How did Paul's actions affect the other kids at school?
7. Can you think of a time when someone was kind to you even when you didn't expect it? How did it make you feel?

Memory Verse

Micah 6:8 "He has shown you, O man, what is good; and what does the Lord require of you? To act justly, to love mercy, and to walk humbly with your God."

Practical Activity: Brick by Brick Discussion

Each child shares one way they can "build" God's Kingdom (like telling the truth, sharing, being kind) and places a paper brick on a wall.

Notes:

LESSON 8: I CAN IMAGINE

Learning Objectives:

By the end of this lesson, children will be able to:

1. Understand that their ability to dream, think creatively, and imagine solutions is a gift from God; and that He has given them a sound mind to think, to plan, and to create (2 Timothy 1:7).

2. Learn that, with God's guidance, no dream is too big to pursue, and that all things are possible when they trust and believe in God's plan for them (Mark 9:23).

3. Understand that God wants them to use their imagination to serve others and make the world a better place, reflecting His love and His care through their creative ideas and actions.

4. Be encouraged to believe in their potential to come up with ideas and solutions that can help others, while relying on God's strength and wisdom to bring those ideas to life.

Story: Isaac's Big Idea

Isaac was a boy full of big dreams. While other kids played games, Isaac loved to sit and think—about the stars, about inventions, and about ways he could make the world a better place.

One day, he told his mom, "I'm going to build a machine that helps people! Maybe it could clean up trash or carry heavy things for the elderly."

His mom smiled and said, "That's a wonderful idea, Isaac! Great things start with imagination, but they come true when you work hard and trust God."

Isaac's eyes lit up. He had never thought of his imagination as something from God. But then he re-membered a Bible verse he had heard in Sunday school: 2 Timothy 1:7(NKJV) — **"For God has not given us a spirit of fear, but of power and of love and of a sound mind."**

"A sound mind," Isaac repeated. "That means God gave me the ability to think, dream, and create!"

From that day on, Isaac started sketching ideas and learning how things worked. He knew some people might laugh at his dreams, but he believed in what Jesus said in Mark 9:23(NKJV): **"If you can believe, all things are possible to him who believes."**

Isaac believed that with God's help, his imagination could become something real—something that could help others and show God's love in action.

And so, Isaac kept dreaming, kept learning, and most importantly—kept believing.

Discussion Questions:

1. What kind of things did Isaac like to think about?
2. What was Isaac's big idea for a machine?
3. What did Isaac's mom say about imagination and trusting God?
4. What does 2 Timothy 1:7 say God has given us?
5. What does having a "sound mind" mean?
6. Why did Isaac keep believing in his ideas, even if people might laugh?
7. How can your imagination be used to help others and

Memory Verse

2 Timothy 1:7 "For God has not given us a spirit of fear, but of power and of love and of a sound mind."(NKJV)

 ## Practical Activity: Dream Cloud Art

1. Kids draw their biggest dream inside a cloud shape.
2. Then each child explains show this can help others.

Notes:

LESSON 9: I AM A KING

Learning Objectives:

By the end of this lesson, children will be able to:

1. Understand that, as followers of Jesus, they are part of God's chosen people—a royal priesthood; with a unique purpose to represent God's light in the world (1 Peter 2:9, Revelation 1:6).

2. Learn that leadership, according to God, is about courage, love, wisdom, and faithfulness, not about physical strength or status. Like David, God chooses those with hearts that trust and obey Him.

3. Realize that they have to master an area, or a certain aspect of life and be king over it.

4. Recognize that God is shaping them to be leaders who reflect His heart and lead with kindness, wisdom, and integrity, just as David led God's people.

5. Feel empowered to stand strong in their faith, knowing that they are chosen by God to be a "king in the making," prepared to lead with love, courage, and honor, reflecting God's

Story: A King in the Making

David wasn't the biggest, the strongest, or even a soldier. He was just a young shepherd boy who loved God with all his heart.

But when he saw a giant, named Goliath, threatening God's people, David didn't run away. While others were afraid, David stepped forward with bravery and faith. He said, "The Lord will help me!" And, with just a sling and a single stone, David defeated the giant!

God saw David's courage and faithfulness. Later, He chose David to be king—not because he was the tallest or the toughest, but because he trusted God with his whole heart. So, David went on to became a wise, kind, and strong leader.

The Bible tells us something amazing: You are also chosen by God!

In 1 Peter 2:9, it says, **"But you are a chosen people, a royal priesthood, a holy nation... to proclaim the virtues of Him who called you out of darkness into His marvelous light."** This means, when you follow Jesus, you are part of God's royal family! You're not just a kid—you're a king in the making, just like David once was.

God is preparing you to lead—not with swords or crowns, but with love, wisdom, and courage.

The Bible says in Revelation 1:6, that Jesus **"has made us to be a kingdom, priests to His God and Father."** And one day, just like it says in Daniel 7:27, **"the greatness of the kingdoms... will be given to the people, the saints of the Most High."**

So, you must choose one thing that you like doing, and learn everything about it, so that you can become a king over that area some day; and God will use you mightily.

Discussion Questions:

1. Who was David before he became a king?
2. What did David do when he saw Goliath?
3. Why did God choose David to be king?
4. What does 1 Peter 2:9 say about people who follow Jesus?
5. What does it mean to be part of God's royal family?
6. How can you show courage and faith like David in your own life?
7. What area will you like to master when you grow up?

Memory Verse

1 Peter 2:9 "But you are a chosen people, a royal priesthood, a holy nation, God's special possession, that you may declare the praises of Him who called you out of darkness into His wonderful light."(NIV)

Practical Activity: King's Crown Craft

1. Boys create their own crowns.
2. Then they write three qualities of a good king on their crowns (like brave, kind, wise).

Notes:

LESSON 10: I AM A QUEEN

Learning Objectives:

By the end of this lesson, children will be able to:

1. Understand that, like Esther, they are chosen and beloved by God. They are royalty in His eyes, with a special purpose to fulfill in His Kingdom, regardless of their background or circumstances (Esther 4:14).

2. Learn that, just as Esther was called "for such a time as this," they too have a unique calling and purpose; and God has placed them where they are to make a difference (Esther 4:14).

3. Grasp that courage, especially when standing up for others or what is right, is an important aspect of being a godly queen, reflecting God's love and justice. They will see that God provides the strength they need in tough situations.

4. Learn that true royalty is not about wearing a crown, but about using one's influence, one's voice, and one's position to help others; and speak up for justice, kindness, and God's love.

5. Be inspired to believe that they, like Esther, can make a powerful impact by trusting in God, and mastering at least one aspect of life to shine His light and help those in need

Story: Queen Esther

A long time ago, in a land called Persia, there lived a young woman named Esther. She wasn't from a royal family—she was an ordinary girl, raised by her cousin, Mordecai, who loved her very much.

Esther loved God, and tried to live in a way that pleased Him. She was gentle, kind, and wise, and her heart was full of courage—even before she knew how much she would need it.

One day, the king of Persia decided to choose a new queen. Many girls were brought to the palace, but Esther stood out—not just because she was beautiful, but because she had a kind and humble spirit. The king chose her to be queen, but Esther kept a secret: she was one of God's people, the Jews.

Sometime later, a dangerous plan was made to hurt the Jewish people. Esther was afraid, but Mordecai reminded her of something very important: "Perhaps you were made queen for such a time as this." (Esther 4:14).

Esther knew she had to do something, even if it was scary. She prayed, she fasted, and she asked God for courage.

Then, she went to the king—something no one was allowed to do without being called. But God was with her. The king listened, and because of Esther's bravery, the lives of her people were saved.

Esther wasn't just a queen because she wore a crown. She was a queen because she used her voice to help others, and stood up for what was right. And you can, too.

God has created you with purpose, and filled your heart with strength, love, and wisdom. Like Esther, you are called to shine His light, speak up with kindness and courage; and make a difference in the world around you.

You may not live in a palace, but in God's eyes, you are royalty—chosen, beloved, and brave.

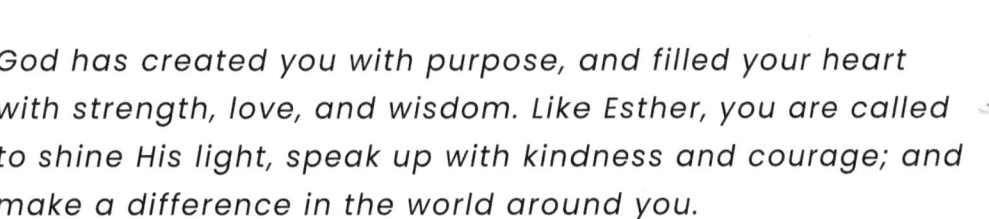

Discussion Questions:

1. Who raised Esther, and what was she like?
2. Why did the king choose Esther to be queen?
3. What secret did Esther keep when she became queen?
4. What danger did Esther's people face?
5. What did Mordecai say that helped Esther be brave?
6. How did Esther show courage?
7. How can you show courage and help others like Esther did?

Memory Verse

Esther 4:14b "And who knows but that you have come to your royal position for such a time as this?(NIV)

Practical Activity: Queen's Crown Craft

1. Girls create their own crowns.
2. Then they write three qualities of a queen on their crowns (like kind, brave, wise).

Notes:

LESSON 11: I AM CREATIVE LIKE MY FATHER

Learning Objectives:

By the end of this lesson, children will be able to:

1. Understand that their ability to imagine, create, and design are special gifts from God, reflecting His own creative nature (Exodus 31:1-5).

2. Learn that just as God filled artists in the Bible with wisdom and skill to create beautiful works, He has also given them unique talents and abilities that can both bring joy to others and honor God.

3. Realize that creativity is not just for fun, but is a way to glorify God and reflect His beauty and order in the world. They are encouraged to use their creativity for good, to serve others, and to show God's love.

4. Be inspired to use their creative skills—whether in art, music, building, writing, or any other form—to serve others and share God's light with the world.

5. Learn that when they create, they are not just making things, but contributing to God's plan of bringing beauty into the world, which honors Him.

Story: Creative Pedro

Pedro loved to draw things, build things with blocks, and imagine amazing inventions.

One day, as he was painting a big rainbow with animals underneath it, he asked his father, "Daddy, how did I get all these fun ideas in my head?" His father smiled, and sat down beside him. "Pedro, your creativity is a special gift from God! When you draw, paint, or build, you are using the talents God has given you. It's one way you can show a little piece of Who He is."

"Really?" Pedro asked, eyes wide with wonder. "Yes," said his father. "Did you know that in the Bible, God gave special gifts to some people to help build His tabernacle—the tent-place where people worshiped Him? God filled them with wisdom and skill so they could make beautiful things for the tabernacle."

Then, his father opened the Bible, and read from Exodus 31:1–5: **"See, I have called by name Bezalel… and I have filled him with the Spirit of God, in wisdom, in understanding, in knowledge, and in all manner of workmanship, to design artistic works…"**

Pedro listened closely as his father continued, explaining how God gave these people the ability to work with gold, silver, jewels, wood, and even fabrics, to make the tabernacle—a very special place to worship God. "Wow," Pedro said, "So God made artists and builders, just like me?" "That's right," his father said. "Just like Bezalel and Aholiab in the Bible, God gave you creative gifts so you can bring joy to others and honor Him."

Pedro looked down at his painting and smiled. "Then, I am going to keep drawing for God!"

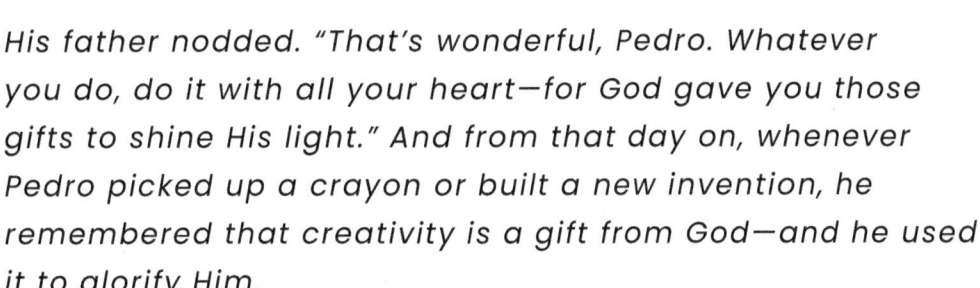

His father nodded. "That's wonderful, Pedro. Whatever you do, do it with all your heart—for God gave you those gifts to shine His light." And from that day on, whenever Pedro picked up a crayon or built a new invention, he remembered that creativity is a gift from God—and he used it to glorify Him.

Discussion Questions:

1. What kinds of things did Pedro like to do?
2. What did Pedro's father say about creativity?
3. Who did God give special creative gifts to in the Bible?
4. What kinds of skills did God give these people?
5. Why do you think God gave people creative gifts?
6. How can you use your own talents and creativity to honor God?
7. What does it mean to "do it with all your heart"?

Memory Verse

Exodus 31:3-5 "I have filled him with the Spirit of God, with wisdom, with understanding, with knowledge and with all kinds of skills—to make artistic designs... to work in gold, silver and bronze, to cut and set stones, to work in wood, and to engage in all kinds of crafts."(NIV)

Practical Activity: Challenge

1. Kids create something (a drawing, a note, or a small gift)
2. Then they give their drawing, note, or craft gift to someone, as a way to share God's love.

Notes:

LESSON 12: I AM BEING TRAINED: TO BECOME A MAN, A HUSBAND, AND A FATHER

Learning Objectives:

By the end of this lesson, children will be able to:

1. Recognize that being a man, a husband, and a father involves not only providing for the family, but also serving, leading by example, and following God's guidance.

2. Understand that true manhood is marked by taking responsibility—whether at home, in relationships, or in their faith—just like David, Daniel, and Jesus did. They will see that working hard and being a servant to others is an essential part of being a strong leader.

3. Learn that growing in wisdom, strength, and favor with God and others is key to becoming a well-rounded man. Like Jesus and the biblical heroes, they are called to grow spiritually and mentally, to be leaders, and to reflect God's love in all they do (Luke 2:52).

4. Grasp that like a godly man leads with love, they show care and sacrifice for others.

5. Be inspired to grow into their future roles as men, husbands, and fathers who will raise their families with love, patience, truth, and godliness (Ephesians 6:4)

Story: Leo and his dad

Leo was a curious boy, who loved spending time with his dad. But, one thing puzzled him: after working all day at his job, Leo's dad would come home and still do chores—fixing things around the house, helping his mom, and even reading Bible stories to Leo and his siblings in the evenings before going to bed.

One day, Leo asked, "Dad, why do you work so hard? Don't you get tired?" His dad smiled, wiped his brow, and sat beside him. "Leo, I do get tired. But being a real man isn't just about working a job or making money. It's about loving my family, leading by my example, and showing you what it means to follow God. This is part of how I serve Him."

Then, his Dad opened the Bible, and shared a few stories.

"Do you remember David?" he asked. Leo nodded. "He fought Goliath!" "Yes," Dad said, "but before he became a king, he was a shepherd. He took care of his father's sheep, learned to play music, and spent time with God. He grew in courage, responsibility, and worship. And the Bible says in 1 Chronicles 11:9(NKJV), **"So David went on and became great, and the Lord of hosts was with him."**

"Or, Daniel and his friends," Dad continued. "They were taken to a faraway land, but they stayed faithful to God.

God gave them wisdom and understanding, and they became leaders in that nation. Then he read from Daniel 1:17(NKJV): **"God gave them knowledge and skill in all literature and wisdom…"**

Leo was quiet, listening closely. "And most of all," his Dad said, "think about Jesus. When He was young, He obeyed His parents, grew in wisdom, and found favor with God and people." He pointed to Luke 2:52: **"Jesus grew in wisdom and strength and in favor with God and people."**

Then Leo's Dad said gently, "When I do the dishes, or fix the door, or pray with you—it's not just to get things done. It's to show you love. Like the Bible says in 1 Timothy 5:8 (ESV) **"If anyone does not provide for his relatives… he has denied the faith."** *Leo's eyes widened. "So you're being a leader like David and Daniel?"*

Dad chuckled. "I'm trying, buddy. Ephesians 5:25 (ESV) says **"Husbands, love your wives, just as Christ loved the church and gave himself up for her."** *"And as your dad," he added, "God wants me to raise you with love, patience, and truth." As Ephesians 6:4(NIV): says,* **"Fathers… bring them up in the training and instruction of the Lord."**

Leo got up, and hugged his dad. "I want to grow up like you, Dad—strong, wise, and full of love."

Discussion Questions:

1. What surprised Leo about his dad when he came home from work?
2. Why did Leo's dad say he works hard, even after his job all day?
3. What did Leo's dad say about David, Daniel, and Jesus?
4. How is Leo's dad trying to be a leader like those Bible examples?
5. What does the Bible say about how husbands should love their wives?

6. What does Ephesians 6:4 tell fathers to do?
7. How can you be a leader like Leo's dad in your own family or school?

Memory Verse

Ephesians 6:4 "Fathers, do not exasperate your children; instead, bring them up in the training and instruction of the Lord."(NIV)

Practical Activity: Daily Responsibility Chart

Boys choose one daily task to complete at home.

Notes:

LESSON 13: I AM BEING TRAINED TO: BECOME A WOMAN, A WIFE, AND A MOTHER

Learning Objectives:

By the end of this lesson, children will be able to:

1. Recognize that women are created to be helpers and supporters, bringing love, peace, and strength to their families; by reflecting God's care and purpose (Genesis 2:18).

2. Learn that tasks like caring for the home, helping family members, and serving with joy are important ways to honor God; and to prepare them for their future roles, as wives and mothers (Colossians 3:23).

3. Understand that growing in love, wisdom, and kindness often happens through the daily responsibilities which God gives them; thus, shaping their hearts for bigger purposes ahead (Proverbs 31:27).

4. Feel motivated to help at home and serve others wholeheartedly, knowing their work is valuable and pleasing to God.

5. Recognize that God is training them now, through everyday moments, to become women who lead with His wisdom, His kindness, and His love.

Story: Lila and her Mom

One sunny afternoon, Lila watched her mom busy at home, sweeping the floor, folding the laundry, and wiping the kitchen counters. She noticed how carefully her mom worked to make everything tidy and peaceful in their home. Then, her mom lit a candle, and smiled as the house filled with a warm, cozy smell.

"Mom," Lila asked, "why do you spend so much time cleaning and organizing the house every day? Isn't it tiring for you?" Her mom sat down, and gently pulled Lila closer.

"It can be tiring, sweet girl," she said, "but I do it with joy. God made women with special gifts. In the Bible, God said it wasn't good for man to be alone, so He made woman to be a helper." Then, she opened her Bible to Genesis 2:18(NIV), and read out aloud: **"The Lord God said, 'It is not good for the man to be alone. I will make a helper suitable for him."**

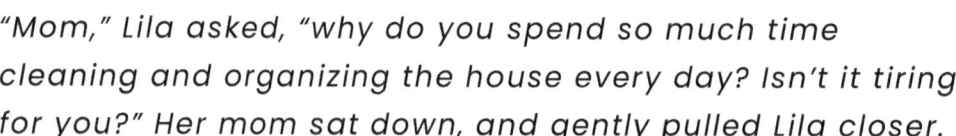

"A helper doesn't mean someone who does everything by herself," Mom explained. "It means being a support—someone who brings peace, love, and strength to the family. One way I do that, is by creating a clean, happy home."

Lila thought about that as she looked around the house. "Does this help God too?" she asked.

Mom smiled. "Yes. God cares about how we serve others—even in small things. When I work with love, I'm not just helping your dad or you and your brother, I'm honoring God."

Then she showed Lila Colossians 3:23: **"Whatever you do, work at it with all your heart, as working for the Lord, not for people."**

Her mom continued, "And one day, you'll have a home of your own. God is preparing your heart now to be wise, kind, and loving." Then, she read Proverbs 31:27(NIV): **"She watches over the affairs of her household and does not eat the bread of idleness."**

Lila's eyes lit up. "So even cleaning is part of what God wants me to learn?" "Yes, my sweet girl," her Mom said. "Just like God gave Daniel and his friends' wisdom, and also trained David to lead, He's shaping your heart through small responsibilities; so, one day, you too can do big things with God's love and His wisdom." Lila smiled, and picked up her toys. "I think I'll start helping right now!"

Discussion Questions:

1. What did Lila notice her mom doing around the house?
2. Why did Lila ask if cleaning was tiring?
3. What did Lila's mom say about being a helper?
4. What Bible verse did Lila's mom read about why God made woman?
5. How does Lila's mom say cleaning and caring for the home honors God?
6. What does Colossians 3:23 teach us about how we should do our work?
7. What does Proverbs 31:27 say about caring for a home?
8. How can small tasks, like cleaning, help prepare us for

Memory Verse

Colossians 3:23 "Whatever you do, work at it with all your heart, as working for the Lord, not for people.

Practical Activity: Helping Hands Pledge

1. Each girl traces her hand on paper.
2. Then, she writes one way that she will use her hands to help others.

Notes:

LESSON 14: I AM CREATED TO BRING LIFE AND BE PRODUCTIVE

Learning Objectives:

By the end of this lesson, children will be able to:

1. Recognize that, like the garden in the story, God created them to grow, produce good things, and make the world better through their gifts and actions (Genesis 1:28).

2. Learn that the gifts, dreams, and kindness God places inside them are like seeds that grow when cared for, like helping others and glorifying God.

3. Understand that by remaining connected to Jesus (John 15:5), they can grow spiritually and produce positive results in their lives and in the lives of others.

4. Appreciate that helping their family, being kind to their friends, and gaining new knowledge; are all ways for them to be productive and honor God.

5. Feel motivated to nurture their abilities and character, so they can "bear good fruit," by reflecting God's love and creativity in their daily lives.

Story: Grandma´s Backyard

One sunny afternoon, Laura went to visit her grandmother in the village. As soon as she arrived, she ran into the backyard, to see the garden. Her eyes grew wide with joy!

SECTION 2: PART 1 - WHO AM I?
LESSON 14: I AM CREATED TO BRING LIFE AND BE PRODUCTIVE

"Wow!" she gasped. "So many colors!" Her Grandmother's garden was full of life. There were big, healthy plants—lettuce, tomatoes, green peppers, onions, chilies, and even some fruit trees. The vegetables looked bright and fresh. It was clear that her Grandmother had taken very good care of everything. "Your garden is so beautiful and full of life, Grandma!" Laura said.

Her Grandmother smiled, and handed Laura a small watering can. "Come," she said. "Let me show you something special." They walked between rows of tomatoes, carrots, and tall sunflowers. Bees buzzed around the flowers, and birds sang nearby.

"Laura," her Grandmother asked, "Did you know that God created us to bring life—just like this garden?" Laura looked at her curiously. "What do you mean Grandma?" Her Grandmother knelt beside a tomato plant, and explained, "In the Bible, God told Adam and Eve to take care of the earth. That means we too, are made to do good things, help others, and make the world a better place."

She opened her Bible again, and read: Genesis 1:28(NIV) – **"God blessed them and said to them, 'Be fruitful and increase in number; fill the earth and subdue it.'"** "Every gift God gives us," her Grandmother said, "is like a seed. When we take care of it, it grows and helps others. Just like I plant seeds in the soil, God plants dreams, talents, and kindness inside of you." She smiled, and added, "When you help your mom, when you are kind to a friend, or when you earn something new, you are being productive. You are using the gifts God gave you."

Then, Grandmother read another verse: John 15:5 says **"I am the vine; you are the branches. If you remain in me and I in you, you will bear much fruit."**

"See?" she said. "When we stay close to Jesus, He helps us to grow. We can do amazing things with His help." Laura looked around the garden, and whispered, "I want to grow good fruit too, Grandma."

Questions:

1. What did Laura see in her grandma's garden?
2. What did Grandma say about how we are like a garden?
3. Which two Bible verses did Grandma read to Laura?
4. What does it mean to "bear fruit," according to the story?
5. How can you stay close to Jesus and keep growing?

Memory Verse

John 15:5 – "I am the vine; you are the branches. If you remain in me and I in you, you will bear much fruit."

 ## Activity:

Write a short reflection: "What kind of fruit is growing in me?" List examples like patience, creativity, kindness, hard work.

Notes:

LESSON 15: I AM CREATED TO CONCEIVE AND GIVE BIRTH TO GOD'S PURPOSE ON THE EARTH

Learning Objectives:

By the end of this lesson, children will be able to:

1. Recognize that God has placed a special purpose inside each of them, to help bring His love, His peace, His truth, and His goodness into the world.

2. Learn that every kind word, helpful deed, and prayer contributes to growing God's Kingdom; just like a seed growing into something big and important.

3. Be inspired by Mary's willingness to say "yes" to God's plan (Luke 1:38); and understand they can also participate by listening, obeying, and trusting God daily.

4. Understand that living out God's love, His kindness, and His truth is how they can actively "conceive" and bring God's purpose to life in their homes, their schools, and their communities.

Story: Anna's Big Idea

Anna read aloud from her Sunday school notebook. "God's purpose for the Earth is to extend His Kingdom on Earth as it is in Heaven."

She was going over her lessons when a big question popped into her heart: "How can I help bring God's Kingdom to Earth?"

She closed her notebook, and went straight to the living room, where her mom was sitting with a cup of tea. "Mom," Anna asked, "how can I help God bring His Kingdom here on Earth?"

Her mom smiled gently and set down her cup. "That's a beautiful question, Anna. God's Kingdom is full of love, peace, truth, and goodness. When we live the way Jesus taught us—by loving others, helping those in need, and sharing the truth—we are bringing His Kingdom to Earth."

Anna turned her head so she could look into her mother's eyes, and asked, "So even the small things I do matter?"

"Yes," Mom nodded. "Every kind act, every honest word, every prayer—it all adds up. God has placed His purpose inside of you. It's like a seed, and when you use your gifts to bless others, you're helping that seed grow."

Luke 1:38(NIV) says, **"I am the Lord's servant," Mary answered. "May your word to me be fulfilled."**

"Just like Mary said 'yes' to God's plan, you can say yes too—by listening to God and obeying Him in small ways every day."

That night, Anna wrote in her notebook: "My big idea: I can bring God's Kingdom to Earth by living like Jesus."

Questions:

1. What big question did Anna ask her mom?
2. What did Anna write in her notebook that night?
3. What do you think it means to give birth to God's purpose?
4. Can children help bring God's Kingdom to Earth? How?
5. What is one gift or idea you have that God could use?

Memory Verse

Luke 1:38 – "I am the Lord's servant," Mary answered. "May your word to me be fulfilled."(NIV)

Activity:

1. Make a crown drawing, titled, "Kingdom of God."
2. Inside their crown, write or draw things they can do to help bring God's Kingdom (for example, pray, forgive, be kind, share God's Word).
3. Write a short journal entry or prayer as follows:
a. Start it with: "God, I want to say Yes to Your purpose.
b. Then, they list the ways they can live out God's Kingdom at home, school, or with friends. End it with: Help me to…"

Notes:

LESSON 16: I AM BEAUTIFUL IN SPIRIT, IN SOUL, AND IN BODY

Learning Objectives:

By the end of this lesson, children will be able to:

1. Recognize that each person is made up of three important parts that work together:
a. Body: interacts with the world through their senses and their physical needs.
b. Soul: includes their mind, their emotions, and their will—how they think and feel.
c. Spirit: their deepest part, that connects with God.
2. Understand why they may feel conflicted inside, and that it's a normal part of being human.
3. Realize that spending time with God through prayer, reading the Bible, and learning His truth strengthens their spirit, helping them to make good choices.
4. Know that they are beautiful because God created their whole being—spirit, soul, and body—and that all three of their parts matter.
5. Commit to developing all the parts of themselves in a balanced and healthy way with God's help.

Story: The Three Dimensions

One day, Linda sat on her bed, looking very disturbed. She was fighting with herself over something she really wanted to do. One part of her thought it wasn't a good idea, but another part really wanted to go ahead. She didn't understand why she was struggling so much inside.

Her father passed by her room and saw her sitting quietly with a frown. He got worried about her, and asked, "Linda, are you okay? Did something happen?"

Linda looked up and said, "I don't know, Daddy. I feel confused. I want to do something, but a part of me says no, and another part says yes. I feel like I'm having a war inside me!"

Her dad sat beside her and smiled gently. "This is actually something we all go through, sweetheart. Every human being has a spirit, a soul, and a body—and sometimes, these don't always agree."

Linda looked puzzled. "What do you mean?"

Her dad explained, "Your body is the part of you that sees, feels, and touches the world. It wants comfort and fun. Your soul is your mind, your will, you're your emotions—how you think and feel. Your spirit is the deepest part of you. That's the part that talks with God."

1 Thessalonians 5:23(NIV) says, **"May your whole spirit, soul and body be kept blameless at the coming of our Lord Jesus Christ."**

"Linda, God made you with all three of these parts, all working together. When your spirit is strong and connected to God, it helps your soul and body make the right choices."

"Wow," Carolina said. "So the struggle I felt was real—but I can learn to listen to my spirit more?"

"Yes!" Her dad smiled. "The more time you spend with God—praying, reading His Word, and learning His truth—the stronger your spirit becomes. It helps you choose what's right, even when it's hard." And remember, God made you wonderfully. You are beautiful in your spirit, your soul, and your body."

Carolina reached over, and gave her dad a big hug.

Thanks, Daddy. I want to grow strong in all three parts of me!"

Questions:

1. What was Carolina struggling with inside herself?
2. Who came in to talk with her?
3. Have you ever felt like your heart and your head were telling you different things?
4. Why do you think God gave us a spirit, a soul, and a body?
5. How can you take care of your spirit, soul, and body this week?

Memory Verse

1 Thessalonians 5:23b – "May your whole spirit, soul and body be kept blameless at the coming of our Lord Jesus Christ."(NIV)

Activity:

1. Draw a picture of a person with three labels:
a. Spirit: heart
b. Soul: brain/feelings
c. Body: hands/feet.
2. Write or draw one way these can take care of each part.
3. Write a short reflection titled: "God Made Me Whole"
4. In it, describe what it means to be beautiful in spirit, soul, and body.
5. Include one goal for each area, for example:
a. Spirit: "Pray every morning"
b. Soul: "Think positive thoughts"
c. Body: "Eat healthy and rest well"

Notes:

LESSON 17: I AM AN ORIGINAL

Learning Objectives:

By the end of this lesson, children will be able to:

1. Recognize that while God has a purpose for all people, each person is given special, original gifts to fulfill that purpose in their own way.

2. Know that they are one-of-a-kind creations, just like fingerprints that are unique to each person.

3. Feel proud and thankful for how God made them—their smile, their voice, their thoughts, and their heart—all God-intended and special.

4. Believe that God did not make mistakes, and that their life has a meaningful role to play in life.

5. Understand that discovering their special talents and gifts is a journey, and that even simple acts like helping or making others laugh are important.

Story: The Special Me

Did you know that as human beings, we all have the same purpose? But each one of us is given a unique gift to fulfill that purpose in a special way.

Never compare yourself to others, because God made you original in your own way.

Think about fingerprints. Each person has a full set of different ones—no two are the same, not even twins who are born on the same day and look exactly alike! Even their fingerprints are different.

You are not ordinary. You are one of a kind! You were made by God with a special purpose that no one else can do like you."

The bible says in Psalm 139:14 (NIV) **"I praise you because I am fearfully and wonderfully made; your works are wonderful, I know that full well."**

"God didn't make a mistake when He made you," Linda's mom said. "He gave you your smile, your voice, your thoughts, and your heart on purpose."

If you are not sure what your gift is yet, don't worry, "You'll discover it as you grow. Sometimes it can be as simple as loving to help, or always making people laugh. So, whenever you stand in front of the mirror, say to yourself with confidence, "I am not a copy of anybody else. I am an original. I am God's special creation."

Questions:

1. What example shows that everyone is made uniquely?
2. Have you ever felt like comparing yourself to someone else? How did it make you feel?
3. What makes you original and different from others?
4. Why is it important to see yourself the way God sees you?
5. What can you say to yourself when you feel "not good enough"?

SECTION 2: PART 1 - WHO AM I?
LESSON 17: I AM AN ORIGINAL

G126 MOVEMENT
BIBLE STUDY PROGRAM
FOR SUNDAY SCHOOL CHILDREN
AGES: 11-12 YEARS

Memory Verse

Psalm 139:14 – "I praise you because I am fearfully and wonderfully made; your works are wonderful, I know that full well."(NIV)

Activity:

1. Write a short letter to themselves beginning with: "Dear Me, I am pleased by the way God made me."
2. Then add: "I am original because…" (Encourage them to list personal gifts, talents, and qualities.)

Notes:

http://www.Treeof-life.com

© TREE OF LIFE

LESSON 18: I SPEAK LIKE MY HEAVENLY FATHER

Learning Objectives:

By the end of this lesson, children will be able to:

1. Understand that words can either build others up or tear them down.

2. Identify times when their words might have hurt others, and feel motivated to change this.

3. Practice using words that encourage, words that bless, and words that help others—just as God speaks, with His love and His power.

4. Realize that people are made in God's image, and so deserve to be spoken to with respect and kindness.

5. Feel how that speaking good words, not only helps others, but also brings happiness and peace to their own heart.

Story: Clemence's Words Matter

Clemence loved to play and laugh with his friends and his little brother, Nathan. But sometimes, Clemence would tease Nathan too much. He'd call him silly names or make fun of him when he made mistakes.

Nathan would frown and look down—but Clemence didn't think much of it.

One day, while playing at a friend's house, Clemence heard his friend's dad talking. "Words are powerful," he said. "They can build someone up or tear them down. God created the whole world with His words—and He wants us to speak like Him: to bless, to heal, and to help."

Clemence's ears perked up. That night, he couldn't stop thinking about it. "My words can hurt or help," he whispered to himself. Then, he remembered what his Sunday School teacher thought them, that life and death are in the power of the tongue … How can we use our tongue to bless our God and Father, and use the same tongue to curse people, who are made in the image of God?

Suddenly, Clemence felt sorry, as he remembered all the times he had made Nathan cry or feel small.

The next morning, when Nathan dropped his cereal spoon, Clemence smiled and said, "It's okay! I'll help you clean it up." Nathan looked surprised—but happy.

That day, Clemence made a choice: He would stop using his words to tease and start using them to bless. Instead, he began saying things like: "You did a great job!" "Thank you for sharing!" "I'm proud of you!"

Every time he spoke kindly, his heart felt lighter. And, Nathan started smiling a lot more.

Questions:

1. What did Clemence like to do with his friends and brother?

1. How did Clemence sometimes treat his little brother, Nathan?
2. What did Clemence hear from his friend's dad, that made him think?
3. What Bible verse did Clemence read about, how we should use our words?
4. How did Clemence feel after reading the Bible verse?
5. What did Clemence do differently the next day?
6. What kind things did Clemence start saying to Nathan?
7. How did using kind words change how Clemence and Nathan felt?

Memory Verse

Proverbs 18:20 - "A man's stomach shall be satisfied from the fruit of his mouth; From the produce of his lips he shall be filled." (NKJV)

Activity: Kind Words Balloon Toss

1. Kids toss a balloon back and forth. At the same time, they say something kind about their partner.
2. If they say something mean or unkind, the balloon "pops" (metaphorically), showing how hurtful words damage relationships.

Notes:

LESSON 19: I AM LOVED BY MY HEAVENLY FATHER

Learning Objectives:

By the end of this lesson, children will be able to:

1. Recognize that God loves them no matter what, even when they make mistakes or feel far from Him.
2. Relate to the biblical story of the lost son who was welcomed back with joy, showing God's forgiveness and mercy.
3. Believe that they are valuable and loved by God and their family, regardless of their failures or imperfections.
4. Develop a heart of thankfulness for the constant and patient love God has for them.
5. Learn that God is always ready to welcome them back when they seek Him, just like the father in the story.

Story: Duarte's Nightmare

Duarte was a thoughtful boy. He liked helping around the house and always tried to be good. But sometimes, he made mistakes—like forgetting to clean up, getting frustrated with his little sister, or talking back when he felt upset.

One day, Duarte sat quietly beside his mom and asked, "Mom… will you still love me if I mess up?" His mom gently hugged him and whispered, "I love you no matter what. Even if you make mistakes, I will always be your mom, and I will always love you."

This made Duarte smile. But in his heart, he still wondered—could anyone really love him no matter what?

At Sunday School that week, Duarte's teacher told a story from the Bible. "It's about a boy who made some big mistakes," she said. "But his father still loved him." Then, she read Luke 15:11–32, the story Jesus told: A man had two sons. One day, the younger son asked for his share of the family's money and left home. He spent all of it doing the wrong things, and soon he had nothing left—not even food. He got a job feeding pigs and was so hungry he wanted to eat the pigs' food!

Finally, he said, 'I'll go home. I'll tell my father I'm sorry and ask if I can work for him like a servant. 'But when he was still far away, his father saw him. And do you know what happened?

He didn't yell or say, "I told you so. "He ran to him, gave him a big hug, and threw a party, because his son had come home. The father said, "This son of mine was lost, and now he is found!"

Duarte's eyes filled with wonder. "Boys and girls," the teacher said gently, "that's how God loves you. Even when you mess up, even when you feel far from Him, He never stops loving you. He's always ready to welcome you back."

That night, Duarte thought about what his mom had said, and what Jesus said too. "My mom loves me no matter what," he whispered. "And God loves me even more." Duarte smiled, closed his eyes, and thanked God. "Thank You for loving me… always."

Questions:

1. What question did Duarte ask his mom?
2. How did Duarte's mom respond?
3. What Bible story did Duarte's Sunday School teacher share?
4. What did the younger son do in the story?
5. How did the father react when the son came home?
6. What does this story teach us about God's love?
7. How did Duarte feel after hearing the story?

Memory Verse

Luke 15:20 - "But while he was still a long way off, his father saw him and was filled with compassion for him; he ran to his son, threw his arms around him and kissed him."(NKJV)

Practical Activity: Love Circle Sharing Time

1. Kids sit in a circle.
2. Then, they share either:
★ one thing they love about God, or
★ one way they feel His love.

Notes:

PART TWO
Why am I Here?

LESSON 20: I AM CREATED IN GOD'S IMAGE AND LIKENESS

Learning Objectives:

By the end of this lesson, children will be able to:

1. Understand what it means to be created in the image and likeness of God, not just physically, but in qualities like His love, His wisdom, His power, and His creativity.

2. Identify the God-like qualities they have been given, such as the ability to create, love, forgive, and think wisely.

3. Explain how their minds reflect God's creativity, and how they can use their imagination for good.

4. Recognize the importance of guarding their thoughts, by choosing positive, life-giving ideas.

Scripture References:
- Genesis 1:26–27
- Proverbs 4:23
- 1 Corinthians 2:16

Comprehension Text:

The Bible says we are created in the image and likeness of God. But what does that really mean? Does God look like us, with two feet and hands? Not exactly.

When God created us, He put everything He is into us in a small way. This means we have some of the same qualities that God has!

- *God is the Creator, and so we can create and imagine.*
- *God is full of wisdom, and we can be wise.*
- *God is love, and we can love others.*
- *God is a King, and we are kings too.*
- *God is compassionate, and we can be kind and caring.*
- *God is all-powerful, and we have power too.*
- *God can forgive, and we can forgive others.*
- *God is creative, and we are creative.*
- *God is Spirit, and we have a spirit too.*
- *God is eternal (forever), and we will live forever too!*

This is what it means when the Bible says we are made in the image and likeness of God. The word "image" can also mean imagination. Our minds are like God's factory where new ideas and creations come from. God sends ideas into our minds to help us create things like books, songs, drawings, inventions, and much more.

The Bible says we have the mind of Christ (1 Corinthians 2:16).

But sometimes, we let bad or negative thoughts fill our minds. Those are lies from the enemy.

Proverbs 4:23 says, **"Be careful how you think, your life is shaped by your thoughts."**

So, we must choose to think good and positive things about ourselves and about others too.

Activity: "God's Image Collage"

1. Create a collage by cutting out pictures or drawing things that show the qualities we share with God, like:
   a. love
   b. wisdom
   c. creativity
   d. kindness.
2. Talk about why each one of these reminds you of God.
3. Homework:
   a. Write or draw one way you can show God's qualities this week (like kindness or forgiveness).
   b. Practice thinking positive thoughts
   c. Memorize Proverbs 4:23, and be ready to share it next Sunday!

Notes:

LESSON 21: I AM CREATED TO HAVE DOMINION

Learning Objectives:

By the end of this lesson, children will be able to:

1. Understand that they were created by God with a unique purpose, which includes having dominion over creation.
2. Explain what it means to have dominion — not as control over people, but as responsibility and care for God's world.
3. Identify the areas in which they can exercise godly authority, such as:
   a. caring for the environment
   b. making wise choices
   c. respecting others.
4. Recognize their identity and value as part of God's plan, regardless of their background or their appearance.

Scripture References:
- Genesis 1:26
- Revelation 22:5
- Psalm 115:16

Comprehension Text:

When a company makes a product, they write down what that product is for—its purpose.

When God made people, He also gave us a clear purpose. Genesis 1:26 tells us that purpose. You are not here by accident! No matter where you were born or your family, God made you for a special reason—to rule, to lead, and to take care of the world around you.

But, this rulership isn't about bossing people around. It means being responsible and taking care of at least one part of God's creation.

The Bible says in Revelation 5:10, **"We shall reign on the earth."** *King David was amazed that God made human beings as rulers over everything He created (Psalm 8:6). Your identity is not about where you come from, or who your family is, or what you even look like. You have God-given authority to:*

1. *Rule the earth for God.*
2. *Have power over the spirit world.*
3. *Take care of the treasures and resources which God put on the earth.*

God gave you a very important job to do in life!

Activity: "My Purpose Crown"

1. Draw or make a paper crown
2. Write or draw on it one way you can be a good leader or caretaker for something God made. It could be either:
a. your family
b. your pets
c. your school, or
d. God's nature around you!

Homework:

1. Think about one way you can take care of something which God gave you this week.
2. Write or draw it in your notebook, as follows:
a. What I will care for: _____
3. Memorize either:
a. Psalm 115:16 or
b. Revelation 22:5
4. Be ready to share about this next Sunday.

Notes:

LESSON 22: MY PURPOSE IS CONNECTED TO THE EARTH

Learning Objectives:

By the end of this lesson, children will be able to:

1. Understand that human beings are uniquely made from both the earth and the Spirit of God, showing their special connection to both the natural world and the spiritual world.

2. Explain that their physical body comes from the earth, which means their purpose is connected to caring for the earth, and living responsibly on the earth.

3. Recognize their dual identity—natural and spiritual — and how this makes them capable of fulfilling God's plan for life on earth.

4. Appreciate that being made from the earth, gives them a reason to respect, protect, and use creation wisely.

Scripture References:
- Genesis 1:20
- Genesis 1:26

Understanding Text:

When God created fish, He spoke to the waters. When He created birds, He spoke to the sky. Genesis 1:20 tells us God commanded the waters to bring forth living creatures, and the sky to be filled with birds. Every creature is connected to the place it came from.

In the same way, when God created mankind, He Spoke to Himself " Let us create man…" God took man from the earth and breathed His spirit into him.

So, part of man was taken from the earth, and part was passed on from God Himself. We are combinations of earth and heaven, natural and spiritual at the same time.

This means we are special—part of us comes from the earth, and part comes from God! But we live in a physical body made from the dust of the ground, because our purpose is connected to Earth!

Activity: "Earth and Spirit Collage"

1. Draw or collect pictures of things that come from the earth (like plants, animals, water), and also things which remind you of spirit or heaven (like clouds, stars, hearts).
2. Glue these on a paper, side-by-side, to show how you are both earth and spirit!

Homework:

1. Find something from nature outside (a leaf, rock, or flower) Then, think about how God used the earth to create life.
2. Write or draw in your notebook:
a. "I am part earth because _____"
b. "I am part spirit because _____"
3. Be ready to share your thoughts about this next Sunday!

Notes:

LESSON 23: I AM A MANAGER AND AN INFLUENCER

Learning Objectives:

By the end of this lesson, children will be able to:

1. Understand that God has made them managers (stewards) of His creation, and that He expects them to take care of what He has given them on this earth.

2. Explain the meaning of being both a faithful and a wise servant, by using their gifts to serve others and to honor God.

3. Recognize their role as influencers—being both salt and light—by making good choices, that positively affect their surroundings.

4. Demonstrate responsibility in practical ways at home, school, and in the community; knowing that their actions can influence others for good and bring glory to God.

Scripture References:
- Luke 12:42–44
- Genesis 1:15
- Matthew 5:13–16

Comprehension Text:

In Luke 12:42–44, Jesus talks about a wise and faithful servant, who takes care of his master's house. When the master comes back, and sees the servant doing a good job, he gives him even more responsibility!

God has given each of us special gifts—not so we can show off or boss others around—but so we can serve and help build His kingdom.

In Genesis 1:15, God put Adam in the Garden of Eden to take care of it. Just like Adam, we are called to take care of everything around us—our homes, nature, and people—by using God's resources wisely.

As God's children, we are managers of this planet. We must take care of the earth and all God has given us.

Some people think there are too many people on earth, but really, there is still plenty of space that needs people to care for it.

In Matthew 5:13-16, Jesus reminds us that we are the salt and the light of the earth. Our good actions should shine and bring glory to God.

Activity: "Manager for a Day"

1. Imagine you are a manager for your home, school, or neighborhood for one day.
2. Draw a picture or write three things you would do, to take care of it and help others.

Homework:

1. Think about a gift or talent God gave you. How can you use this to help others, or take care of something around you?

2. Write or draw your answer in your notebook:

a. "My special gift is _____, and I will use it to _____."

3. Practice saying Matthew 5:16(AMP): *"Let your light shine before others, so that they may see your good deeds and glorify your Father in heaven."*

Notes:

LESSON 24: I AM A BUILDER AND A REPAIRER

Learning Objectives:

By the end of this lesson, children will be able to:

1. Understand that God calls them to be builders and repairers—people who help fix what is broken in the world around them.
2. Explain the example of Nehemiah, and how taking the initiative, can lead to positive change in their community or their relationships.
3. Recognize that being a repairer isn't just physical rebuilding, but also includes helping others, healing relationships, and spreading hope.
4. Identify practical ways they can bring healing and restoration to their homes, schools, and neighborhoods; through their kindness, through their service, and through their leadership.

Scripture References:
- Nehemiah 2:17–18
- Isaiah 58:12

Comprehension Text:

Isaiah 58:12b(NKJV) tells us, **"You shall be called the Repairer of the Breach."** *This means God calls us to help fix things that are broken. Sometimes that means helping to rebuild walls, sometimes it means fixing relationships with others, or it means helping our community become better.*

In Nehemiah 2:17-18, Nehemiah saw the walls of Jerusalem were broken and in need of repair. Instead of waiting for someone else to do this, he took action himself, and began rebuilding the walls. We are called to be like Nehemiah—to be builders and repairers wherever we go.

We can bring healing, hope, and restoration to broken places and broken hearts by the way we act and by the way we love others.

Activity: "Fix It!"

1. Think about something that may be broken or not working well in your home, school, or community (like a friendship, a broken toy, or a messy room).
2. Draw a picture of it,
3. Then draw how you can help fix or rebuild it.

Homework:

1. Think of one way you can help fix or improve something around you this week.
2. Write or draw your plan in your notebook.
3. Share with your family or friends how you want to be a builder and repairer.

Notes:

LESSON 25: I AM CALLED TO LEAD

Learning Objectives:

By the end of this lesson, children will be able to:

1. Understand that God has called them to be leaders in the world, starting with how they act at home, at school, and in their communities.

2. Explain that godly leadership means leading with kindness, fairness, and a servant heart—like Jesus.

3. Recognize that when righteous people lead, it brings peace and joy; and that they have a role to fulfill in making the world better, through their leadership.

4. Identify areas where they can show leadership now, and be inspired to take on leadership roles in future with confidence and godly character.

Scripture References:
- Genesis 1:28
- Proverbs 29:2

Understanding text:

God wants His children to be leaders! From the very beginning, God gave human beings the job of taking care of the earth. This means, we are called to be rulers—not in a bossy way—but by being kind, by being fair, and by leading like Jesus.

When God made Adam, He told him to take care of the earth (Genesis 1:28). This means we are all supposed to be leaders in different areas—at school, in our communities, and even in big jobs like being the president, the mayor, or the governor.

The Bible says in Proverbs 29:2(NKJV), **"When the righteous are in authority, the people rejoice; but when the wicked man rule, the people groan."**

This means when good people lead, everyone is happy. But when bad people lead, life becomes hard. So, God wants His children—you and me—to be in charge, and to bring joy and peace wherever we go!

Activity: "God's Leader Badge"

1. Draw a big badge or medal on your paper.
2. Inside the badge, write: "Called to Lead"
3. Decorate it with your favorite colors and symbols of leadership (like a crown, a world globe, ...).
4. Cut it out
5. Wear it proudly—or put it on your wall, to remind you that you're a leader for God!

Homework: My Leadership Plan

1. Write down or draw three ways you can be a good leader this week. Here are some ideas to help you:
   a. Help a classmate at school
   b. Tell the truth, even when it's hard
   c. Pray for your town or country's leaders
2. Bring your plan next Sunday, and share what you did!

Notes:

LESSON 26: I CAN SUBDUE AND OVERCOME

Learning Objectives:

By the end of this lesson, children will be able to:

1. Understand what it means to subdue and overcome challenges, both outside (like problems or people) and inside (like fear or negative thoughts).
2. Explain that God has given them the strength and power to overcome evil with good, as taught in Romans 12:21.
3. Recognize that their identity in God makes them strong, wise, and capable of facing hard situations with courage and faith.
4. Apply this truth by choosing positive actions and thoughts, when facing difficulties or doubts in daily life.

Scripture References:
- Romans 12:21
- Philippians 4:13
- 2 Timothy 1:7

Understanding Text:

God made you strong! This means, you can overcome (win against) things that try to stop you from doing what God wants. To subdue, means to make something obey—even when it's hard.

Sometimes we face problems in nature, like storms or sickness. Sometimes we struggle inside, like with bad thoughts, fear, or feeling like we're not good enough. But guess what? You can overcome all of that!

The Bible says in Romans 12:21(NKJV) **"Do not be overcome by evil, but overcome evil with good."** *That means, when something bad tries to pull you down—like anger, fear, or a mean person—you can beat it by choosing to do what is good and right with God's help.*

Even when negative thoughts come to your mind—like "I'm not smart enough," or "I'll never be great"—God says you can subdue those thoughts by remembering who He says you are: strong, wise, and full of His power!

Activity: "Overcomer Shield"

1. Draw a big shield on your paper.
2. Inside the shield, write: "I Am an Overcomer!"
3. Around the shield, draw or write things you want to overcome (like fear, anger, laziness, …).
4. Then cross those out and write what you will use to overcome them (like prayer, kindness, courage).
5. Color and decorate your shield—then hold it up like a superhero!

Homework: Speak Life Challenge

1. This week, every time a negative thought comes to your mind, speak a truth from God's Word instead! Here are a few examples:

a. When you think: "I can't do this," say: "I can do all things through Christ" (Philippians 4:13).

b. When you feel scared, say: "God has not given me a spirit of fear" (2 Timothy 1:7).

2. Write down two negative thoughts you had this week

3. Then, write down what truth from God's Word you used to fight them.

4. Bring your note along next Sunday.

Notes:

LESSON 27: I AM CALLED TO EXCEL AND GROW

Learning Objectives:

By the end of this lesson, children will be able to:

1. Understand that God wants them to grow spiritually, grow up mentally, and grow in their actions, just as Jesus did.
2. Explain that growth requires effort from them—learning, listening to God's Word, and following Jesus every day.
3. Recognize that growing in grace, knowledge, and good works is part of living a life that pleases God.
4. Identify practical ways they can choose to grow in their faith, in their character, and in their abilities in their daily lives.

Scripture References:
- 2 Peter 3:18
- Colossians 1:10

Understanding Text:

God wants us to grow, and get better, just like a good father wants his children to grow up strong and wise. Many kids grow up to do what their parents do, like becoming teachers, builders, or leaders.

In the same way, we are God's children, and He wants us to do what He does, like showing love, helping others, leading with kindness, and growing in wisdom.

2 Peter 3:18(NKJV), says *"Grow in the grace and knowledge of our Lord and Savior Jesus Christ."*

But, to grow, we need to learn new things, listen to God's Word, and follow Jesus every day. Growth doesn't just happen by accident—we must choose to grow in our thinking, in how we act, and in how much we know God.

Colossians 1:10(NKJV) says *"Walk worthy of the Lord, fully pleasing Him, being fruitful in every good work and increasing in the knowledge of God."*

Even Jesus took time to grow in His body, in His knowledge, and in His relationship with God and people. And since we're following Him, we must grow too!

Activity: "My Growth Tree"

1. Draw a big tree with lots of branches.
2. At the bottom (the roots), write: "I belong to God."
3. On each branch, write or draw something you want to grow in (like:
   a. prayer
   b. kindness
   c. reading the Bible
   d. helping others,
   e. learning at school).
4. Decorate your tree with:
   a. fruit
   b. leaves, or
   c. flowers, to show how growth brings good things!

Homework: Grow One Step This Week!

1. Choose one area where you want to grow (spiritually, emotionally, or mentally).
2. Write it down or draw a picture of it.
3. Then each day this week, do one thing that helps you grow in that area. For example:
4. Want to grow in kindness? Do one kind thing each day.
5. Want to grow in your faith? Read your Bible or pray every morning.
6. Bring your growth step or drawing back next Sunday.
7. Tell the class what you learned this week!

Notes:

LESSON 28: I CAN BE PRODUCTIVE AND FRUITFUL

Learning Objectives:

By the end of this lesson, children will be able to:

1. Understand that God's command to be fruitful, means to use their gifts, talents, and their time to create and produce good things.
2. Explain that being fruitful goes beyond only having children—it includes making a positive impact in the world through their actions and creativity.
3. Recognize that they have the mind of Christ, which helps them think wisely and be productive.
4. Identify ways to use their unique gifts and opportunities to grow and contribute to God's kingdom and the world around them.

Scripture References:
- Genesis 1:28
- John 15:16
5. 1 Corinthians 2:16

Comprehension Text:

Did you know that the first command God gave to human beings, was to be fruitful? This means, God wants us to grow, to create, and to produce good things with our lives!

In Genesis 1:28(NKJV), God said **"Be fruitful and multiply, and fill the earth and subdue it."**

Being fruitful doesn't just mean having children—it means using what God gave you to make something good! This includes your mind, your time, your talents, and your heart. Jesus also said in John 15:16(NIV), **"I chose you and appointed you so that you might go and bear fruit—fruit that will last."**

You have something special inside you—an idea, a talent, a gift—that God wants to grow.

Many people stay poor or stuck because they don't use what God already gave them. But you are not like that! You have the mind of Christ (1 Corinthians 2:16), which means you can think wisely, you can create, and you can be productive.

Activity: 'My Fruit Basket of Gifts"

1. Draw a big basket on your paper.
2. Inside your basket, draw or write different kinds of fruit.
3. On each fruit, write one of the following:
a. gift
b. talent, or
c. idea that God has given you (like singing, drawing, helping, inventing, praying, building, thinking).
4. Decorate your basket and
5. Thank God for making you fruitful!

Homework: Use Your Gift This Week!

1. Pick one fruit (gift or idea) from your drawing basket.
2. Find a way to use that gift or idea to bless someone this week! For example:
   a. If your gift is drawing, make a card to cheer someone up.
   b. If your gift is helping, do a kind chore without being asked to do it.
3. Write or draw what you did.
4. Bring it next Sunday to share how you were fruitful!

Notes:

LESSON 29: I AM HERE TO ESTABLISH AND RESTORE

Learning Objectives:

By the end of this lesson, children will be able to:

1. Understand that God created them with the ability and purpose to establish (start) and restore (fix) things in the world around them.

2. Explain that being part of God's work means, helping to build up what is broken, and making positive changes; instead of complaining or giving up.

3. Recognize that their actions can support healing and restoration in their homes, their communities, their schools, and their churches.

4. Identify ways they can partner with God, by starting new, good things, or supporting others who do so.

Scripture Reference: John 3:17

Understanding Text:

God made you to build things and fix things! That's part of His image in you.

Just like God made and restored the earth in Genesis, you also have the power to create, to establish (start), and to restore (fix) what is broken.

Sometimes people feel frustrated or sad when they aren't able to build or finish something that matters to them—because it's in us to want to do good and make a difference.

But, instead of just complaining when things go wrong, God wants us to be people who help make things better!

The Bible says in John 3:17(NIV) **"For God did not send His Son into the world to condemn the world, but to save the world through Him."**

So, instead of making things worse, like the devil wants, we partner with God to build up and restore what is broken.

You may be called to help fix a broken home, school, community, or church—or to start something new, like a business or ministry! Even if you're not the one who starts it, you can always support others doing such good work.

Activity: "Role Play"

Scene: Teens Group Classroom

Teacher: Hi everyone! Today's lesson is about something very powerful—that God created you to establish and restore. This means you're here to start good things, and fix broken things, in your world. Sounds exciting, right?

Teacher: Let's start with a little role play to help us understand this better. I will need a few volunteers! (Teacher selects 3 or 4 volunteers)

Role Play Setup

Teacher: Okay, here's the situation: Imagine our classroom is a community. Sometimes, things are great, but sometimes things get broken or need help—like when someone is sad, or when there is a mess to clean up, or when something new needs to be started.

I'll give you roles, and you'll act out the scene. Ready?

Scene 1: The Broken Playground

Teacher: (to Student 1) You are a kid who sees that the playground equipment is broken and dangerous. What do you do?

Student 1: I tell the teacher or adults about the broken swings, so they can fix them.

Teacher: Great! That is noticing a problem. Now, (to Student 2), you are a friend who feels upset because the playground is broken. What can you do to help?

Student 2: I can talk to my friends about taking care of the playground, and help clean up the area around it.

Teacher: Awesome! And (to Student 3), you're a leader, who decides to start a playground safety team. How do you encourage others?

Student 3: I ask my classmates to join me, and then we make posters about keeping the playground safe.

Discussion:

Teacher: What did we see happening in this role play? (Pause for answers)

Student 4: Someone noticed something broken, and told others.

Student 5: Others helped fix or clean it, and someone started something new like a safety team.

Teacher: Exactly! That's restoring, fixing what's broken, and establishing or starting new, good things.

Scene 2: At Home—Fixing a Problem

Teacher: Let's try one more! (to Student 2), you see your sibling is upset, because they feel left out of a game. What can you do to restore peace?

Student 2: I can invite them to play with me and my friends, and so make sure everyone feels included.

Teacher: Yes! And (to student 1), how can you help establish something new at home?

Student 1: Maybe I can start a family game night, so everyone has fun together.

Wrap-Up Discussion

Teacher: See how your actions—starting good things, or helping fix problems—can bring healing and joy? God wants you to be part of His work by establishing and restoring.

Interactive Question Time

Teacher: Who can share one way you think you can start something new, or you could fix something broken at school, at home, or at church?

(Encourage 3 or 4 responses)

Student 3: I want to help my class by starting a kindness club.

Student 4: I'm going to help clean up trash in our Kingdom School playground.

Closing Prayer

Teacher: Let's thank God, for giving us the ability to establish and restore things. I'll pray, and you can all say "Amen" when I finish.

"Dear God, thank You for making each of us able to start new, good things and fix broken things. Help us to see what needs to be restored around us, and give us the courage to act. Let us be part of Your work in our homes, in our schools, and in our communities. Amen."

Homework: Be a Restorer This Week!

1. Ask God to show you one thing that needs fixing or helping, and do something about it! For example:
a. Help clean a messy area at home or school.
b. Encourage someone who feels down.
c. Say something kind, instead of complaining.
2. Write down what you did, or draw a picture of it.
3. Then, bring it along next Sunday.
4. Share with your class, how you partnered with God to restore something.

Notes:

LESSON 30: I HAVE GIFTS AND TALENTS

Learning Objectives:

By the end of this lesson, children will be able to:

1. Understand that God has given each of them unique gifts and talents to use for His purposes.
2. Explain how Moses used his God-given gifts to accomplish great things, even when he felt unsure.
3. Recognize different kinds of gifts—natural abilities and spiritual gifts—and that all are important.
4. Identify ways to use and grow their gifts, to help others, and serve God faithfully.

Scripture Reference: 1 Peter 4:10

Comprehension Text:

Moses was chosen by God for a very important job, to lead the people of Israel out of slavery in Egypt.

At first, Moses didn't feel ready. He was shy and unsure. But God had given Moses special gifts to help him. These included performing miracles, leading people, and doing amazing signs and wonders. Moses used his gifts to do what God called him to do!

Just like Moses, you also have gifts and talents from God. Some may be natural, like drawing, singing, or playing sports.

Others may be spiritual, like praying for others, or teaching the Bible. Some gifts grow as you practice them, and others come from the Holy Spirit.

Sometimes people are afraid to use their gifts, just like the man in Jesus' story who buried his one talent. But, God wants us to use our gifts to help others and to grow! The more you use what God has given you, the more He will trust you with even more gifts!

Activity: "Gift Hunt"

1. On a piece of paper, write down or draw five gifts or talents you believe God has given you. They can be anything—like:

   a. helping your friends

   b. reading

   c. cooking

   d. drawing, or

   e. singing.

2. Then, ask a friend or family member to tell you one gift they see in you too! You might be surprised by what they say!

Homework: Use Your Gift This Week!

1. Choose one of your gifts, and use it to bless someone else this week. For example: If your gift is kindness, write a kind note to someone.

2. Write or draw in your notebook what you did, and how it felt.

3. Memorize 1 Peter 4:10.

4. Be ready to share your memory verse in class next Sunday!

Notes:

LESSON 31: I AM A PROBLEM SOLVER

Learning Objectives:

By the end of this lesson, children will be able to:

1. Understand that God created them with unique gifts and ideas, to solve problems in the world.

2. Explain how problem-solving can bring help and hope to others, just like the biblical heroes did and everyday inventions do.

3. Recognize that their feelings about issues around them may be a sign of their purpose to make a difference.

4. Identify ways they can use their talents and ideas to solve problems and show God's goodness to others, regardless of their age or size.

Scripture Reference: Matthew 5:14

Understanding Text:

God made you special with your own gifts, talents, and ideas because He knew the world would need someone just like you to help solve problems.

Think about it:

- *Jesus solved the biggest problem ever—sin!*
- *Joseph in the Bible, solved the problem of famine in Egypt.*
- *Cars solve the transportation problem.*
- *Clothes solve the problem of being cold or uncovered.*

Guess what? You were born to solve a problem too!

Maybe, you care about animals, you care about helping others, or making people laugh, or protecting nature. When something makes you feel angry, sad, or bothered, that may be a clue that God wants to use you to help fix it.

When you solve problems for others, it makes people see how awesome and good God is. This why you should never think you are too young or too small to make a difference!

Activity: "Problem Busters"

1. Think of one problem in the world or your community, that makes you feel sad or upset.
2. Then, draw or describe how YOU would solve this with your talents and gifts.
3. You can decorate it like a superhero plan!

Homework: My Problem-Solving Plan

1. This week, look for one small problem you can help solve, like:
a. helping a friend
b. picking up trash, or
c. sharing with someone who needs it.
2. Ask an adult what school subjects or skills you need to learn more about in order to help solve your big problem one day.
3. Write it down or tell your teacher:
a. What bothers me: _____
b. How I want to help: _____
c. What I want to learn: _____

4. Then, don't forget to memorize Matthew 5:14 for next Sunday.

Notes:

LESSON 32: I AM FEARLESS

Learning Objectives:

By the end of this lesson, children will be able to:

1. Understand that fear is a common challenge, but it doesn't come from God.

2. Explain that God gives them power, love, and self-discipline, instead of fear (based on 2 Timothy 1:7).

3. Recognize that trusting God helps them overcome fears, and step into the purpose He has for them to do.

4. Identify ways to face fears with faith and with courage, knowing God supports and loves them unconditionally.

Scripture References:
- 2 Timothy 1:7
- Philippians 4:13

Comprehension Text:

Did you know that fear is the number one thing that tries to stop people from living the life God planned for them?

God has amazing plans for you, plans that take faith and courage. But sometimes, fear tries to whisper things like:

- *"You're not good enough."*
- *"You might fail."*
- *"What if people laugh at you?"*

But, God says something very different! He says: "I did not give you a spirit of fear. I gave you power, love, and self-discipline."

God wants you to trust Him, and not be afraid. He's not waiting to punish you if you make a mistake. He's a kind, loving, Father Who helps you learn and grow.

When you break free from fear, a whole new world of possibility and purpose opens up to you. You can do what God has called you to do!

Activity: "Fear-to-Faith Flip Chart"

1. Take a piece of paper and divide it in half.
2. On the left side, write or draw something you're afraid of.
3. On the right side, write or draw what God says about it in His Word. For example:
a. Left – "I'm afraid to speak in front of people."
b. Right – "God gives me courage. I can do all things through Christ!" (Philippians 4:13)
4. Decorate your chart.
5. Keep your chart to remind yourself: You are fearless!

Homework: Fearless Mission Challenge

1. This week, ask God to help you be brave in one small way. (Maybe it's trying something new, talking to someone, or standing up for what's right.)

2. At home, write or draw a short note:
a. What I was afraid of: _____
b. What I did anyway: _____
c. How God helped me: _____
3. Memorize 2 Timothy 1:7, and be ready to say it next Sunday.

Notes:

LESSON 33: I AM PART OF A BIGGER PICTURE

Learning Objectives:

By the end of this lesson, children will be able to:

1. Understand that each person is a unique and important part of God's bigger plan, just like pieces of a puzzle.
2. Explain that as part of the Body of Christ, they have a role to play in their family, in their church, and in their community.
3. Recognize that working together and caring for others helps build stronger, kinder relationships.
4. Identify ways they can support, love, and serve those around them as part of God's family.

Scripture Reference: Romans 12:5

Understanding Text:

Imagine a big puzzle. Each piece is different, but every piece is important to make the whole picture complete.

God made each of us like a living stone, unique and special, and He wants us to work together like a big family called the Body of Christ.

Just like in your family, everyone has a role to play. Sometimes families have problems, but problems don't break the family—they help us learn to be stronger and kinder.

When we only think about ourselves, we forget how important it is to help and care for others. God wants us to think about our family and community—to share, support, and love each other.

Activity: "Body of Christ Puzzle"

1. Draw a big body shape on a piece of paper.
2. Write your name on one part (like an arm or a foot).
3. Ask your classmates or family members to write their names on other parts.
4. Talk about how every part is needed to make the body work!

Homework: Family & Friends Challenge

1. This week, do one kind thing to help your family or friends.
2. Write or draw in your notebook:
a. What I did to help my family or friends: _____
b. How it made me feel: _____
3. Memorize Romans 12:5.
4. Be ready to share your memory verse next Sunday!

Notes:

LESSON 34: I MAKE A DIFFERENCE

Learning Objectives:

By the end of this lesson, children will be able to:

1. Understand that God made them to make a difference in the world, not just to go to heaven.

2. Explain that their talents and gifts are tools to create, help, and bring God's kingdom to earth.

3. Recognize that using their gifts, even when they are still learning, can impact others and honor God.

4. Identify ways they can actively choose to make a positive difference in their families, in their schools, and in their communities.

Scripture Reference: Ephesians 2:10

Understanding Text:

The people in the Bible knew exactly why God made them. Their goal wasn't just to get to heaven; they wanted to make a difference here on earth, before they died.

God gave you hands and gave you talents, so that can do amazing things! Your hands can create, help, build, and even perform miracles when used for God's kingdom.

Sometimes, we don't use our gifts because we haven't learned how yet. But when we discover what God has called us to do and start using our gifts, we will make a powerful difference for God's glory!

Let's work together to take back what the enemy has tried to steal, like joy, peace, and hope; and honor God, by doing His will here on earth, just like it is in heaven.

Activity: "My Helping Hands"

1. Trace your hand on a piece of paper.
2. Inside each finger on your paper, write one way you can use your hands to help others or make a difference.
3. Decorate your hand drawing.
4. Share your drawing with your family or class!

Homework: Purpose in Action

1. Think of one thing you want to do to make a difference to this week.
2. Tell an adult or friend your plan and ask for their help, if you need it.
3. Write or draw in your notebook:

a. What I want to do: _____

b. How I will do it: _____

4. Memorize Ephesians 2:10.
5. Be ready to share your memory verse next Sunday.

SECTION 2: PART 2 - WHY AM I HERE?
LESSON 34: I MAKE A DIFFERENCE

Notes:

LESSON 35: I NEED WISDOM AND HELP

Learning Objectives:

By the end of this lesson, children will be able to:

1. Understand that true wisdom begins with them trusting and respecting God.
2. Explain that God's wisdom helps them make good choices, plan well, and build a better life.
3. Recognize that the Holy Spirit is their Helper, Who guides and supports them when they ask for His help.
4. Identify practical ways to seek God's wisdom, and ask for the Holy Spirit's help with their daily decisions and their challenges.
5. Scripture References:
- Romans 11:33
- John 14:26

Understanding Text:

King Solomon was the wisest and richest man in the Bible. Did you know that your own success and happiness are connected to how much wisdom you have?

God's wisdom and riches are so amazing, we can never fully understand them. But He wants us to use the wisdom He gives us to make good choices, to prepare, to plan, and to build things that help us live better.

The Bible says, "The fear of the Lord is the beginning of wisdom." This means, when we respect and trust God, we start to become wise.

When you need help, God's Spirit is right beside you! Jesus called Him the Helper.

The Holy Spirit won't help, unless you ask. So, when you feel stuck, just say, "Holy Spirit, please help me," and He will guide you.

Activity: "Ask the Helper"

1. Draw a picture of yourself, with a speech bubble saying, "Holy Spirit, please help me!"
2. Write or talk about one thing you want God's help with this week.
3. Keep your drawing to remind you to always ask for His help!

Homework: Wisdom Walk

1. Think of one decision you need to make this week.
2. Pray and ask the Holy Spirit for His wisdom.
3. Write or draw in your notebook:
   a. What I asked the Holy Spirit to help me with: _____
   b. What happened after I asked Him: _____
4. Memorize John 14:26.
5. Be ready to share your memory verse next Sunday.

Notes:

LESSON 36: I AM A BLESSING

Learning Objectives:

By the end of this lesson, children will be able to:

1. Understand that God created them to be a blessing to others, not just for themselves.
2. Explain the process of growing like a fruit tree—planting seeds, growing, and then producing fruit to bless others.
3. Recognize the importance of patience and trust in God's timing as they grow and bless those around them.
4. Identify ways they can be a blessing to their family, their friends, and their community through their actions and attitudes.

Scripture Reference: Matthew 28:19

Understanding Text:

God created you to be a blessing to others. Sometimes, God shows us the result like helping many people; but He doesn't always explain how it will happen. We need to be patient, and trust Him, as we work through this process.

Think about fruit growing on a tree.

- *To get fruit, you need a seed.*
- *The seed must be planted in the right ground.*
- *The tree grows and then produces fruit.*
- *The fruit has seeds to grow more trees.*

The tree doesn't grow fruit just for itself—it grows fruit to bless others! To help others learn and grow, we have to be a blessing to them first.

Activity: "Fruit of Blessing"

1. Draw a tree with fruit on it.
2. On each fruit, write one way you can be a blessing to your family, your friends, or your community.
3. Share your tree with someone, and talk about how you want to bless others!

Homework: Plant a Seed of Blessing

1. This week, do one kind thing to bless someone (help, share, encourage).
2. Write or draw in your notebook:
a. How I blessed someone: _____
b. How it made me feel: _____
3. Memorize Matthew 28:19
4. Be ready to share your memory verse next Sunday.

Notes:

LESSON 37: I PROTECT AND CARE

Learning Objectives:

By the end of this lesson, children will be able to:

1. Understand that God gave human beings the important responsibility to take care of the earth and to protect it.

2. Explain why caring for the environment is like taking care of something valuable, like a family car or a toy.

3. Recognize that taking care of God's creation is a continuous and important job for everyone of them.

4. Identify practical ways they can protect and care for the earth in their daily lives.

Scripture Reference: Psalm 115:16

Comprehension Text:

God gave us a very special gift: the earth, and everything we need to live comes from it: the food we eat, the water we drink, and the air we breathe.

The Bible says that while heaven belongs to God, He gave the earth to us, His children. This means, it's our job to take care of the planet, and protect it, just like taking care of a toy you own.

Think about your family car—if you don't take care of it, it can break down or get ruined. But if you take care of it by fixing it and keeping it clean, it lasts a long time. It's the same with the earth!

God gave Adam the job of caring for the garden. It wasn't just a small task; it was a big, important job that needed to be done all the time. We also have that same responsibility to protect God's creation.

 Activity: "Earth Helpers"

1. Draw a picture of the earth
2. Then, around it, write or draw three ways you can help protect and care for God's creation. For example: picking up trash, saving water, planting trees.

Homework: Care for Creation Challenge

1. This week, do one thing to help take care of the earth.
2. Write or draw in your notebook:
a. What I did to help the earth: _____
b. How it made me feel: _____
3. Memorize Psalm 115:16.
4. Be ready to share your memory verse next Sunday.

Notes:

LESSON 38: I REBUILD RELATIONSHIPS

Learning Objectives:

By the end of this lesson, children will be able to:

1. Understand that their true worth comes from their relationship with God, not from outward things.

2. Explain the importance of having close, loving relationships with their family and their friends.

3. Recognize that when relationships are broken, this can affect their happiness and their life.

4. Identify ways to take responsibility for rebuilding peace and love in their relationships, by following God's command to love others.

Scripture References:
- Luke 10:27
- Romans 12:18

Understanding Text:

God created you as His special child. Your true worth and who you are comes from your relationship with Him—not from how you look, what you do, or where you come from.

We have a body from our parents, but our spirit, our real self comes from God. When we don't have a good connection with God, we may feel like something is missing or empty inside of us.

God also made us to have close relationships with other people, especially family and friends. When our relationships are not right, it can make life harder and less happy. Romans 12:18 says **"If it is possible, as much as depends on you, live peacefully with all men".**

The most important command God gave us, is to love Him with all our heart and to love others just like we love ourselves. Everything in God's kingdom works best when we live in love and good relationships.

Activity: "Heart Connections"

1. Draw a big heart in the middle of a piece of paper.
2. Around it, draw smaller hearts.
3. Then, write the names of people you love—family, friends, teachers, God.
4. Think about ways you can show love to these people this week.

Homework: Love in Action

1. Pick one person this week you want to show love to in a special way.
2. Write or draw in your notebook:
   a. Who I want to love better: _____
   b. What I will do: _____
   c. How it made me feel: _____
3. Memorize Luke 10:27
4. Be ready to share your memory verse next Sunday.

Notes:

LESSON 39: I AM CREATED TO RULE IN MY AREA

Learning Objectives:

By the end of this lesson, children will be able to:

1. Understand that God created everyone with a unique purpose and calling.
2. Explain that their gifts and talents can open doors and create opportunities, just like David's did.
3. Recognize the importance of practicing and developing their gifts in order to grow in their influence and in their leadership.
4. Identify ways they can take responsibility to lead, and make a difference in their own area of life.

Scripture References:
- Proverbs 18:16
- Proverbs 22:29

Understanding Text:

God created every person with a purpose that is the same for all humans. But the way you live out that purpose, is different from everyone else, because your calling and gifts are unique.

The Bible says that your gift can open doors for you, and bring you before important people!

Take David, for example. His job was to take care of sheep, but David was wise—he used his free time to practice and discover his gifts.

One day, because of those gifts, he was brought before the king, and given a great opportunity.

God wants you to practice and grow your gifts. When you do, you will have influence and be able to lead in your own special way.

Activity: "Role-play"

Scene: Sunday School

Teacher: Hey everyone! Today, we're going to learn something really important — that God created each of us with a special purpose. And, just like David in the Bible, each of us has gifts and talents that can open doors for us and help us lead in our own areas.

Teacher: Can anyone tell me, who David was, and what made him special?

Student 1: David was a shepherd boy, who became king. He was brave and trusted God.

Teacher: Exactly! David's gifts—like his courage, his skill with a sling, and his heart for God—all helped him to lead and to make a difference. Even before he was king, he was practicing those gifts every day.

Teacher: Now, let's try a quick activity! I want everyone to take a minute to think quietly about three gifts or talents you have. These can be anything: sports, drawing, being kind, making friends laugh, or even listening well.

(Pause for 30 seconds for reflection)

Teacher: Alright! Would anyone like to share with us just one of the gifts they thought about?

Student 2: I'm good at drawing.

Student 3: I like helping people.

Teacher: Those are fantastic! Now, let's do something fun. I'm going to hand out some cards with different everyday situations written on them—like "Helping a new student," "Organizing a group project," or "Cheering someone up." I want you to think about how your gift could help you in that situation.

(Teacher hands out cards, and then gives the kids a couple minutes to think about it)

Teacher: Who wants to share their card, and how they might use their gift in that situation?

Student 4: I got "Helping a new student." Since I'm good at making people laugh, I could make the new student feel welcome, by being friendly and funny.

Student 5: Mine says "Organizing a group project," and since I like sorting and putting things in order, I can take charge to help the group stay on track.

Teacher: Awesome! That's exactly what leadership looks like—using your gifts to help others, and take responsibility.

Teacher: Now, here's a quick challenge: Think of one way you can practice your gift this week. Maybe it's helping at home, encouraging a friend, or trying something new in a club or class.

(Allow a moment for thinking)

Teacher: Who wants to share their challenge with us?

Student 2: I'm going to draw talking images, to teach little children about God's kingdom.

Student 3: I'm going to try to help my little brother with his homework, even if it's hard.

Teacher: That's wonderful! Remember, like David, you are getting ready to lead in your own special way. God gave you those gifts on purpose, so you can make a difference right where you are.

Closing Prayer

Teacher: Let's finish with a quick prayer, asking God to help us discover and grow our gifts.

(Teacher leads the prayer)

"Dear God, thank you for creating each of us with special gifts. Help us to discover those gifts, to use them well, and to lead with courage and kindness like David did. Guide us to make a difference in our families, schools, and communities. Amen."

Notes:

LESSON 40: I REPRESENT GOD'S KINGDOM

Learning Objectives:

By the end of this lesson, children will be able to:

1. Understand that everything God created reflects His greatness and His glory.
2. Explain how Jesus represented God's kingdom by showing God's love, His healing, and His kindness.
3. Recognize that they are called to represent God's kingdom through their actions and words.
4. Identify ways to live as ambassadors for Christ, showing God's love and truth in their daily lives.

Scripture References:
- Psalm 19:1
- II Corinthians 5:20

Comprehension Text:

Everything God made shows how wonderful He is—the stars, the sky, the earth, and even you!

The Bible says the heavens declare the glory of God. This means God's greatness is visible all around us.

Jesus showed God's glory by the amazing things He did. When people saw Jesus helping, healing, and loving others, they saw God's kindness and His power.

Jesus wants us to represent God's kingdom by doing good things that make God look good. Our actions should help others see God's love and His power through us.

God sent Jesus to save us and bring back His kingdom on earth. Now, God's people, you and I, are called to represent Him everywhere, showing His love and truth to the world.

"Now then, we are ambassadors for Christ, as though God was pleading through us: We implore you on Christ's behalf, be reconciled to God". II Corinthians 5:20

 Activity: "Glory Mirror"

1. Draw a big mirror on your paper
2. Then, inside your mirror, write or draw ways you can show God's glory to others.
3. Think about how your actions can reflect God's love and kindness every day!

Homework: Shine for God

1. This week, do one good thing that shows God's love to someone.
2. Write or draw in your notebook:
a. What I did to represent God's kingdom: _____
b. How it made me feel: _____
3. Memorize Psalm 19:1.
4. Be ready to share your memory verse next Sunday.

Notes:

LESSON 41: CREATION IS WAITING FOR ME

Learning Objectives:

By the end of this lesson, children will be able to:

1. Understand that Jesus came to restore all creation, and we have the job to continue His work.
2. Explain that their unique role—whether big or small—is to show Jesus' love and His truth to the world.
3. Identify ways to be "light and salt" by showing Jesus' character in their daily lives.

Scripture References:
- Romans 8:19
- Matthew 5:5

Comprehension Text:

When Adam and Eve disobeyed God, it affected the whole world—plants, animals, and people.

But, Jesus came to save and restore everything that was broken. He did His part, by paying the price with His blood; and now He has given us the job to finish the work He began.

Your special calling, no matter what job or role you have—whether a doctor, a parent, a teacher, or a minister—is to show Jesus to the world.

All creation is waiting for God's children to show His love and His truth. God wants us to become more like Jesus in how we live and treat others.

When you read about people in the Bible—kings, prophets, shepherds, and warriors, they all showed parts of Jesus' character. They helped reveal Who Jesus is.

We don't need to shout or scare people to tell them about Jesus. Instead, we can be like light and salt. Showing His kindness, His love, and His truth through our words and actions. That is how we reveal God's glory to the world.

 Activity: "Light and Salt"

1. Draw a candle and a salt shaker.
2. Write or draw ways you can be like light and salt to your family, your friends, and your neighbors this week.

Homework: Shine Jesus' Light

1. Think of one way you can show Jesus' love this week.
2. Write or draw in your notebook:
a. How I will show Jesus: _____
b. What happened when I showed Jesus: _____
3. Memorize Romans 8:19.
4. Be ready to share your memory verse next Sunday!

Notes:

PART THREE
Where did I come from?

LESSON 42: I COME FROM GOD

Learning Objectives:

By the end of this lesson, children will be able to:

1. Understand that God is our Source, and that we come from Him.
2. Know that God created the world and made people to live in it to take care of it.
3. Explain how God gave life to Adam, by breathing His spirit into him, making Adam alive.
4. Realize that they carry God's life and His goodness inside them, because they are made in God's image.

Comprehension Text:

God is our Source—this means we came from Him. He created the whole world, and then He made people to live in it to take care of it.

He made us to be like Him and to do things that reflect Who He is—like loving, creating, helping, and leading.

When God made Adam, the first person, He formed his body from the dust of the ground. But Adam didn't become alive until God breathed His own breath into him. That breath gave Adam his spirit—his real life— and it came directly from God!

This means, you carry something very special inside of you—God's own life and goodness. You are made in God's image, and you are here to reflect Him in your words, your actions, and your love for others.

Questions:

1. What does it mean that "God is our Source"?
2. How did God make the first person, Adam, come alive?
3. What are some ways we can show that we are made like God?
4. What does it mean to be made in God's image?
5. Can you think of something kind or helpful you've done, that reflects God?
6. What makes you feel special about coming from God?
7. How can we show God's goodness to people at school, at home, or in our neighborhood?

Scripture References:

1. *Genesis 1:27(NKJV) "So God created mankind in His own image, in the image of God He created them; male and female He created them."*

2. *Genesis 2:7(NKJV) "Then the Lord God formed the man from the dust of the ground. He breathed the breath of life into the man's nostrils, and the man became a living person."*

Activity: My Real Source Poster

1. Write the title: "I come from God!"
2. Draw or paste pictures of things you enjoy doing (like helping, drawing, singing, or playing with others).
3. Around the pictures, write or draw ways you can use those gifts to reflect God (for example, "I sing to make people happy," "I help my parents at home").

Notes:

LESSON 43: I COME FROM HEAVEN

Learning Objectives:

By the end of this lesson, children will be able to:

1. Understand that they are more than just kids on Earth—they come from Heaven and were created by God for a special purpose.
2. Recognize that before they were born, they were with God; and God sent them to Earth on a mission.
3. Explain that their mission is to bring God's love, His kindness, and His light into the world right now.
4. Realize that they are God's hands, His feet, and His voice on Earth; and God can use them to help and speak to others.

Comprehension Text:

Did you know you are more than just a kid living on Earth? Even though we were born here, the Bible says that we come from Heaven!

Before you were born, you were with God. You were in His heart. He made you for a very special time and place—right now, right here! God sent you to Earth on a mission to bring His love, His kindness, and His light into the world.

This means you're not here by accident. You came from Heaven, sent by God, to help bring His Kingdom to Earth. Every time you forgive, love, share, or speak the truth— you're helping God's Kingdom grow right where you are.

You are God's hands, His feet, and His voice on Earth. If He wants to help someone, He can use you. If He wants to speak to someone, He can speak through you. That's how important you are!

Questions:

1. How does it feel to know that God made you for a special time and place?
2. What kind of mission did God send you on?
3. Why do you think God wants to use you to help others?
4. What does it mean to be God's hands, His feet, and His voice on Earth?
5. Do you think God planned something special for your life? Why, or why not?
6. What can you do this week to show God's love to someone around you?

Scripture references:

1. **Jeremiah 1:5** *"I knew you before I formed you in your mother's womb. Before you were born, I set you apart..."*

2. **Ephesians 2:10** *"For we are God's handiwork, created in Christ Jesus to do good works, which God prepared in advance for us to do."(NIV)*

Activity: "Heaven Mission Badge"

1. Draw and cut out a circle or shield shape.
2. Write: "Citizen of Heaven – On Mission for God!"
3. Decorate it with symbols of Heaven (like hearts, light, a crown, or a dove).
4. Wear or display your badge this week to remind yourself: "I come from Heaven, and I'm here on a mission!"

Notes:

LESSON 44:
I COME FROM THE KINGDOM OF HEAVEN

Learning Objectives:

By the end of this lesson, children will be able to:

1. Understand that God planned the Earth so His heavenly Kingdom could grow.

2. Recognize that, like princes and princesses, they belong to God's royal Kingdom.

3. Explain that God has given each of them a special job as royal messengers, to show His love, His kindness, and His truth on Earth.

4. Learn that the Kingdom of Heaven gives them power—like keys—to pray, believe, and follow God's ways to make good changes.

5. Realize that even though they live on Earth, they come from the Kingdom of Heaven; and are called to share God's love with others.

Comprehension Text:

A long time ago—even before the world was made—God planned to create the Earth so that His heavenly Kingdom could grow.

When we believe in Jesus and follow Him, we are "born again." This means, we become part of God's family and a citizen of the Kingdom of Heaven.

Just like a prince or princess belongs in a royal kingdom, we belong in God's heavenly kingdom.

God gave each of us a special job to do while we live here on Earth. We are like royal messengers, sent to show God's love, His kindness, and His truth to others.

Jesus also told us that the Kingdom of Heaven gives us power—like keys—to help make good changes on Earth. These "keys" mean that we can pray, we can believe, and we can follow God's ways to help others and make the world better.

Even though we live on Earth, we came from the Kingdom of Heaven—and we get to share His love with everyone around us.

Questions:

1. What kind of jobs did God give us to do on Earth?
2. What are some ways we can show love and kindness to others?
3. What do the "keys" to the Kingdom of Heaven help us do?
4. How can praying help us make good changes in the world?
5. Why do you think God wants us to be messengers of His Kingdom?
6. Can you think of a time when you helped someone like Jesus would?
7. How does it feel to know you're part of God's royal family?

SECTION 2: PART 3 - WHERE DID I COME FROM?

LESSON 44: I COME FROM THE KINGDOM OF HEAVEN

G126 MOVEMENT
BIBLE STUDY PROGRAM
FOR SUNDAY SCHOOL CHILDREN
AGES: 11-12 YEARS

Bible references:

1. *John 3:3 Jesus replied, "Very truly I tell you, no one can see the kingdom of God unless they are born again."(NIV)*

2. *Matthew 16:19 "And I will give you the keys of the Kingdom of Heaven. Whatever you forbid on earth will be forbidden in heaven, and whatever you permit on earth will be permitted in heaven."*

Activity: "Heaven's Kingdom Passport" Craft

Goal: Fill your passport with acts of love that show you belong to the Kingdom of Heaven!

1. Write your name on the cover, and title it "Citizen of Heaven".
2. On the inside, draw pictures of ways you can serve God this week (like helping others, praying, reading the Bible, or telling a friend about Jesus).
3. Each day, color in one picture as you complete that action!

Notes:

LESSON 45: I AM A KINGDOM AMBASSADOR

Learning Objectives:

By the end of this lesson, children will be able to:

1. Understand what an ambassador is, and how they represent their home country in another place.
2. Recognize that God created people to represent Him in order to show others what He is like.
3. Describe how, like ambassadors, they bring the culture of God's Kingdom—His peace, His love, His truth, and His light—into the world around them.

Comprehension Text:

For example, if someone is from America, but lives in another country as an ambassador, they speak and act on behalf of their home country.

Did you know that you are an ambassador too? When you follow Jesus, you become a Kingdom Ambassador—someone who represents God's Kingdom here on Earth!

God created people to represent Him and show others what He is like. He gives us special jobs to do, like sharing His love, being kind, telling others about Jesus, and living the way God wants us to live.

When a kingdom sends an ambassador to a new place, they want to bring the culture of their kingdom into that land. That's just like what we do for God's Kingdom—we bring His peace, His love, His truth, and His light to the world around us!

Scripture Reference:

***Matthew 28:19** "So go and make followers of all people in the world. Baptize them in the name of the Father and the Son and the Holy Spirit."*

Questions:

1. What is an ambassador?
2. Who do we represent when we follow Jesus?
3. What kind of mission does God give His ambassadors?
4. What are some ways you can be a Kingdom Ambassador this week?

Activity: "Ambassador Badge" Craft

1. Cut out a badge shape
2. Write on it: "Kingdom Ambassador for Jesus"
3. Decorate your badge with symbols like a crown (for God the King), a heart (for love), or a world globe (for the world).
4. Wear it during the week
5. Remember: everywhere you go, you represent God's Kingdom!

SECTION 2: PART 3 - WHERE DID I COME FROM?
LESSON 45: I AM A KINGDOM AMBASSADOR

Notes:

LESSON 46: I AM DESIGNED BY GOD ALMIGHTY

Learning Objectives:

By the end of this lesson, children will be able to:

1. Understand that God is the greatest artist, Who designed and created each of them on purpose.
2. Know that every part of them—their smile, their voice, their mind, and their personality—were all made specially by God.
3. Recognize that God made them while they were still in their mother's tummy; and that they are not a mistake.
4. Realize that comparing themselves to others is not helpful, because everyone is different; like different tools that have different important jobs.

Comprehension Text:

Did you know that God is the greatest artist of all time? He made you! Every part of you—your smile, your voice, your mind, and even your personality—was made on purpose by God.

God made you while you were still in your mother's tummy. He didn't make a mistake. He made you special because He has a job just for you—something only you can do! Maybe you're good at helping others, drawing, speaking kindly, solving puzzles, or leading your friends. Those are all gifts God gave you.

Sometimes we get into trouble when we compare ourselves to others. But, that's like comparing a spoon to a paintbrush—both are important, but they do different things!

God created us to:

- Do good work
- Grow and learn
- Show His goodness
- Be strong and brave
- Act like Him
- Represent Him on Earth
- Do the special jobs He gave us to do

You are God's masterpiece, designed for a big purpose!

Bible reference:

Psalm 139:14 "I praise you because you made me in an amazing and wonderful way."

Questions:

1. Who made you, and how did He make you?
2. Why did God give you special talents and gifts?
3. What happens when we compare ourselves to others?
4. Can you name one thing God made you good at?

Activity: "God's Masterpiece Mirror" Craft

1. Glue your mirror or foil to the center of your paper.
2. Around it, write words that describe how God made you special (for example creative, kind, brave, joyful).
3. At the top, write: "God's Masterpiece!"
4. Hang it somewhere to remind you: God designed you with love and purpose!

Notes:

LESSON 47: I AM SKILFULLY AND WONDERFULLY MADE

Learning Objectives:

By the end of this lesson, children will be able to:

1. Understand that God made every part of them with great skill and care, like a master artist.

2. Recognize that they were made wonderfully, from their head to their toes.

3. Explain that their hands and abilities can do amazing things when they learn and practice.

4. Realize that God put great potential (hidden power or ability) inside them, but they need to learn, train, and work hard to grow.

5. Understand that God wants them to do their best in everything—in school, at home, and by helping others—and that their excellence points others to God.

6. Know that they are full of purpose, and that the world needs the gifts God gave them.

Comprehension Text:

God made every part of you with great skill and care. He didn't just throw you together—He designed you like a master artist would have done. From your fingers to your brain, from your heart to your smile—you were made wonderfully!

Your hands alone can do so many amazing things, if you learn and practice. You can play music, write stories, paint pictures, build things, create new things, help someone up, or bake cookies.

But, your hands can also learn bad habits—so, that's why we must use our hands wisely, to do what is right and helpful. God put so much potential (that means hidden power or ability) inside you! But to grow and become all God made you to be, you must be willing to learn, train, and work hard.

God wants His children to be excellent in everything—at school, at home, and even when helping others. When you do your best, others notice, and it points them to the God Who made you!

You are full of purpose, and the world needs what God has placed inside of you!

Scripture Reference:

Proverbs 22:29 "Do you see a person skilled in his work? He will serve kings. He will not serve someone who is unimportant."

Questions:

1. What does it mean to be "skilfully and wonderfully made"?
2. What are some amazing things your hands can do?
3. Why is it important to use your hands for good?
4. How can you grow and become all God wants you to be?

Activity: "Hand of Potential" Craft

1. Trace your hand on a piece of paper.
2. Inside each finger, write or draw one thing you can do well or want to learn (like draw, help, cook, play piano, or build).
3. At the top, write: "My Hands Were Made for Great Things!"
4. Decorate it.
5. Hang it up where you can see it every day.

Notes:

LESSON 48: I NEED THE KINGDOM OF GOD

Learning Objectives:

By the end of this lesson, children will be able to:

1. Understand that the Kingdom of God is a place where God is in charge, and where we can find peace, joy, and everything we need.
2. Recognize that we were made to live in God's Kingdom and to help build it.
3. Explain that when people ignore God's Kingdom, problems like struggles in families, conflicts between countries, and false teachings happen.
4. Realize that the Kingdom of God is the solution to the problems we face in the world.

Comprehension Text:

There is a place where we can find peace, joy, and everything we need! That place is called the Kingdom of God! It is a place where God is in charge.

King David said in the Bible, that his biggest wish was to be close to God all the time. Why? Because in God's presence, we find what our hearts are really looking for!

We were made by God to live in His Kingdom, and to help build it here, on Earth. This means bringing God's love, His truth, and His goodness into our families, our schools, and our neighborhoods.

But, when people leave out the Kingdom of God, things go wrong—families struggle, countries argue, and schools teach things that aren't true. That is why we need God's Kingdom, as it is the solution to all the problems we have in our world.

Scripture Reference:

***Psalm 27:4** "I ask only one thing from the Lord. This is what I want: Let me live in the Lord's house all my life. Let me see the Lord's beauty and look with my own eyes at his Temple."*

Questions:

1. What is the Kingdom of God?
2. What happens when people leave the Kingdom of God?
3. What is one way you can help build God's Kingdom this week?

Activity: "Kingdom Builders Challenge"

1. Create a chart with 7 boxes—one for each day of the week.

2. In each box, write or draw one way you can help build God's Kingdom (examples: pray for someone, help at home, read the Bible, learn a skill, master your gift).

3. Each day, check off/tick or decorate a box when you complete a "Kingdom action."

4. Goal: By the end of the week, you'll have done 7 things to help show God's Kingdom to the world.

Notes:

LESSON 49: GOD SENT ME TO DO HIS WORK

Learning Objectives:

By the end of this lesson, children will be able to:

1. Understand that God had a plan for their life before they were born, and they were created on purpose for a purpose.

2. Recognize that many people work hard, but feel unhappy, because they are not doing the work God send them to do.

3. Know that God promises to take care of them, so they don't need to worry and can focus on their calling.

4. Realize that God's Kingdom is inside them; and that by doing God's work, others can see His Love and Power through them.

5. Believe that they are never too young to do great things for God, and can start right now.

Comprehension Text:

God had a plan for your life before you were even born! you're not here by accident—you were created on purpose, for a purpose!

Some people spend their whole lives just trying to make money or just to survive, but they forget the most important thing—the work God gave them to do. They work and work, but they're not happy, and they don't feel fulfilled. That's because they're not doing what God created them to do.

But here's the good news: God promises to take care of us, so we don't have to worry all the time. That way, we can focus on our calling—the special work God has for us to do.

Even as a kid, you have a calling! You can love others, you can tell people about Jesus, you can help your family, you can be a good friend, or you can use your talents for God. God put His Kingdom inside of you, and when you do the good things He made you to do, the world sees His love and His power through you! You're not too young to do great things for God. Start now!

Bible reference:

Ephesians 2:10 "God made us. He created us in Christ Jesus to live good lives. He planned these good things for us long ago."

 Activity: "Role Play - Discovering My God-Given Purpose"

Materials Needed:

- Paper or cards with different "callings" or "jobs" written on them (like love others, share Jesus, help family, be a good friend, use talents).
- Space for acting.

Roles:

- Story-teller
- Kid 1, Kid 2, Kid 3 (each with a different calling)
- Worried Person (feels unsure about his or her purpose)
- God (optional role)

Script/Role Play Instructions:

- **Story-teller**: "Before you were born, God had a plan just for you! You weren't made by accident. Everyone has a special work God wants them to do."

- **Worried Person**: "But I'm just a kid! How can I do anything important?"

- **Kid 1** (holding a card that says "Love Others"): "I can love my family and love my friends every day. That's part of God's work for me!"

- **Kid 2** (holding a card that says "Share Jesus"): "I can tell others about Jesus and what He's done. That's my special job."

- **Kid 3** (holding a card that says "Use Talents"): "I'm good at drawing and helping people, so I use my talents to serve God."

- **God** (optional, with arms open): "I made you for a purpose, and I will help you do the work I've given you. You're never too young to make a difference!"

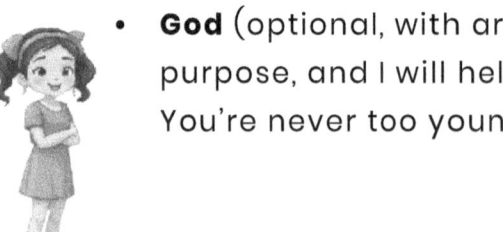

- **Worried Person** (smiling): "Wow! I didn't know I could do important things for God right now. I want to start today!"

- **Narrator** (closing): "God sent each of us with a special job to do. When we use our gifts and love for Him, we show His power and His light to the world!"

Discussion Questions after role play:

1. What are some special jobs God gave you?
2. Why is it important to know that God has a plan for your life?
3. How can you start doing God's work today?
4. Who can help you with your calling?

Notes:

LESSON 50: NOBODY ELSE CAN DO WHAT I DO

Learning Objectives:

By the end of this lesson, children will be able to:

1. Understand that God made them special and unique—there is no one else exactly like them.
2. Know that God gave them a special job, that only they can do, even if others have similar talents.
3. Recognize that they are part of God's royal family, chosen to do important work for Him.
4. Realize that they are never too small or too young to matter in God's big plan.
5. Believe that when they use their gifts for God, they shine His light into the world.

Comprehension Text:

God made you special. You are one of a kind—there's no one else in the whole world exactly like you! God gave you a special job that only you can do.

You may have the same talents as someone else, but no one can use those talents exactly the way you do. The Bible says you are part of God's royal family, chosen to do important work for Him.

God created human beings to rule and take care of the Earth. That means, He gave you the ability to make good choices, solve problems, create new things, and be a leader for what is right.

So, never think you're too small or too young to matter. What you do matter—and how you do it—is very important to God's big plan. When you use your gifts for Him, you shine His light into the world!

Bible reference:

Psalm 8:6 "You put humans in charge of everything you made. You put all things under their control."

Questions:

1. What makes you special in God's eyes?
2. What does it mean to be part of a "royal family"?
3. Why is it important to use the gifts God gave you?
4. Can anyone else do your job in God's plan?

Activity: "God's Special Assignment Card"

1. On the front of your paper, write: "Nobody Else Can Do What I Do!"
2. On the back, write or draw 3 things you are good at or ways you can serve God (examples: singing, helping, praying, leading, creating).
3. Decorate your card.
4. Keep your card somewhere special, to remind you of how important you are to God's Kingdom.

Notes:

LESSON 51: GOD NEEDS ME ON THIS EARTH

Learning Objectives:

By the end of this lesson, children will be able to:

1. Recognize that God gave human beings the job to take care of the Earth and use its resources wisely.

2. Explain that the Bible tells us to rule over the fish, the birds, the animals, and over everything on the Earth; which means we have both responsibility and power to take care of the world.

3. Realize that to take care of the Earth and build God's Kingdom, they need to work hard, they have to think creatively, and they have to use the gifts God gave them to do so.

4. Believe that God wants to work through them to make the Earth a better place.

Comprehension Text:

God made the Earth full of amazing things—fish, birds, animals, trees, rocks, metals, and so much more! But guess what? None of these things will do anything for us unless we work with them.

Imagine if trees could just build you a house all by themselves—wouldn't that be cool? But we have to use our hands, brains, and creativity to make such things happen. That is because God gave us the job to take care of the Earth and use what's in it wisely.

In the Bible, God told us to rule over the fish, the birds, the animals, and over everything on the earth. This means we have responsibility and power to take care of the world and use its resources wisely in order to help people and build God's Kingdom.

But we can only do this if we work hard, think creatively, and use all the gifts God gave us. God wants to work through you to make the Earth a better place!

Scripture References:

1. **Genesis 1:28(NKJV) "Then God blessed them, and God said to them, 'Be fruitful and multiply; fill the earth and subdue it; have dominion over the fish of the sea, over the birds of the air, and over every living thing that moves on the earth.'"**

2. **Colossians 3:23(NKJV) "And whatever you do, do it heartily, as to the Lord and not to men."**

Questions:

1. What did God ask human beings to do with the fish, the birds, and the animals?
2. Why don't things like trees or metals just build things by themselves?
3. How can you use your creativity and energy to help take care of the Earth?
4. What does it mean that God wants to work through you?

Activity: "Earth Keeper" Project

1. Write a list of ways you can help take care of the Earth (examples: planting a tree, recycling, saving water, helping animals).

2. Pick one thing from your list to do this week.

3. If you want, create a small craft or drawing using recycled materials to show how you can use what God gave you to care for the planet.

Notes:

LESSON 52: THE EARTH IS MY PERMANENT HOME

Learning Objectives:

By the end of this lesson, children will be able to:

1. Understand that God created the Earth as a beautiful and special home for us to live, to grow, and to enjoy life.

2. Know that Earth was meant to be our forever home where we walk with God and take care of His creation.

3. Recognize that sin, which began when Adam disobeyed God, separated us from God and made the world feel less like home.

4. Learn that God sent Jesus to show us the way back to our true home—the Kingdom of God.

5. Realize that the Bible teaches we will live and reign on Earth forever with Jesus, making Earth our permanent home.

Comprehension Text:

When God created the Earth, He made it as a beautiful and special home for us. He filled it with trees, rivers, mountains, animals, and everything we would need to live, grow, and enjoy life. It wasn't just a place to visit—it was meant to be our forever home, where we would walk with God and take care of His creation.

*But something sad happened. A long time ago, when Adam disobeyed God. That choice brought sin into the world.
Sin is anything we do that goes against God's ways, and which separated us from Him. It's like getting lost in your own neighborhood—everything looks familiar, but it doesn't feel like home anymore.*

Even now, we sometimes feel that something is missing. You can have fun, toys, games, even lots of friends, but your heart might still feel empty inside. That's because our spirits were made to live with God, not separated from Him.

The good news is this: God didn't give up on us. He sent His only Son, Jesus, to show us the way back to our true home—The Kingdom of God.

When we follow Jesus, we begin to live the Kingdom way— showing God's love, showing His kindness, showing His forgiveness, and showing His truth. And as we grow in Him, we start to feel at home again, even when the world around us isn't quite perfect yet.

Some people think our forever home is just in the sky or far away in heaven. But the Bible says something amazing in Revelation 5:10 , **"God has made us kings and priests... and we shall reign on the earth."** *And, Matthew 5:5 says,* **"Blessed are the meek, for they shall inherit the earth."** *So guess what? The Earth is not just where we live for now. It's where we'll live forever with Jesus our King.*

Bible references:

1. **Revelation 5:10 (NKJV)** "And have made us kings and priests to our God; and we shall reign on the earth."

2. **Matthew 5:5 (NKJV)** "Blessed are the meek, for they shall inherit the earth."

Questions:

1. Who made the Earth? Why did He make it?
2. What happened that made people feel separated from God?
3. Who did God send to bring us back to Him and teach us about His Kingdom?
4. According to Matthew 5:5, who will inherit the Earth?
5. What does Revelation 5:10 say we will be on Earth one day?

Activity: "My Forever Home"

Group Recitation Instructions (for 4 Kids)
Roles:

- **Kid 1**: Verses 1 & 2
- **Kid 2**: Verses 3 & 4
- **Kid 3**: Verses 5 & 6
- **Kid 4**: Verses 7 & 8
- **All Together**: The final verse

Recitation

- **Kid 1**: God made the Earth with love and light,
  ★ Trees, stars, and rivers shining bright.
  ★ He made a home for all to share,
  ★ With animals and skies so fair.

- **Kid 2**: But then came sin, when man went wrong,
  ★ And sadness took the place of song.
  ★ Still, God had a loving plan,
  ★ He sent His Son to help each man.

- **Kid 3**: Jesus came full of love,
  ★ He brought the Kingdom, a gift of hope.
  ★ When we choose to walk His way,
  ★ He fills our hearts with joy each day.

- **Kid 4**: So Earth is more than just a place,
  ★ It's where we'll live in God's embrace.
  ★ And we will live with Jesus there,
  ★ Forever home, beyond compare!

- **All Together**:
  ★ With joy and love our hearts will sing,
  ★ We'll live forever with our King!

Notes:

More Books & Resources

DISCIPLING NATIONS SERIES

Kingdom Mandate (for any donation)
Discovering the Lost Kingdom (Volume 1) $14.00
Purpose, Calling, and Gifts (Volume 2) $15.00
God's Original Design (Volume 3) $20.00
Seeing, Entering, and Manifesting the Kingdom of God (Volume 4) $20.00
The Ekklesia (Volume 5) $30.00
The Gospel of the Kingdom (Volume 6) $20.00
Power and Authority of the Church (Volume 7) $15.00
Kingdom Family (Volume 8) $15.00
The Birthing of a Kingdom Nation (Volume 9) $20.00
What Happened to God? (Volume 10) $20.00
7 Dimensions and Operations of the Kingdom of God (Volume 11) $15.00
Kingdom Economy (Volume 12) $15.00
Kingdom Government (Volume 13) $15.00
Releasing Kings and Queens into God's Original Intent (Volume 14) $10.00
Kingdom Secrets to Restoring Nations Back to God (Volume 15) $20.00
Keys to Fulfilling Your Kingdom Assignment (Volume 16) $20.00

KINGDOM LIVING SERIES

The Three Most Important Decisions of Your Life $15.00
Recognizing God's Timing for Your Life $12.00
Overcoming the Spirit of Poverty $10.00
Seven Kinds of Believers $10.00
7 Dimensions of God's Glory $5.00
7 Dimensions of God's Grace $10.00
7 Kinds of Faith $8.00

HEALING OF THE NATIONS SERIES

Principles of Self Governance $20.00

KINGDOM BOOKS FOR KIDS

Genesis 126 Three Volume Book set for boys $25.00
Genesis 126 Three Volume Book set for boys $25.00
Genesis 126 Coloring Books for Boys $15.00
Genesis 126 Coloring Books for Girls $15.00

GENESIS 126 TEACHER'S MANUAL

Level 1 6-8 years $15.00

G126 MOVEMENT
BIBLE STUDY PROGRAM
FOR SUNDAY SCHOOL CHILDREN
AGES: 11-12 YEARS

© TREE OF LIFE

Level 2 8-10 years $15.00
Level 3 10-12 years $15.00

TO PLACE AN ORDER:

www.TheKingdomNetwork.org
Phone: 1-800-558-5020
Email: info@TheKingdomNetwork.org

Are you struggling to discover your **PURPOSE ?**

You are not supposed to fit in but stand out !

Sign up today for the FREE Online Kingdom Course

DISCOVERING

THE LOST KINGDOM

In this course you'll DISCOVER:

>> Your true identity and purpose

>> What God is doing on the earth and how you can partner with Him in it

>> Why God created the earth and put us on this planet

>> And much more ...

Why are people becoming more and more disinterested in **church and religion** globally? Join the course, and discover **what your soul has been searching for all along.**

FREE BOOK AND STUDY GUIDE

Other courses available

>> DISCOVERING PURPOSE, CALLING AND GIFTS

>> SEEING, ENTERING AND MANIFESTING THE KINGDOM

>> GOD'S ORIGINAL DESIGN

>> The Ekklesia

>> The Next move of GOD

And more ...

Register Now @ **www.TheKingdomUniversity.org**

Welcome to
KINGDOM DELIVERANCE
— WORKSHOP —

Are you tired of waiting and looking for breakthroughs? Kingdom of God has the answer.

This kingdom deconstruct workshop is divided into EIGHT major categories which deal with the seven major areas of our life. Each one is connected to the next, and so if one of these areas dysfunctions, it will affect all other areas of your life.

1. Relationship with the Father
2. Spiritual Healing
3. Emotional Healing
4. Purpose and Calling
5. Mastering Gifts and Skills
6. Finances—Learning to Live in Kingdom Economy
7. Healing Relationships
8. Physical Health

Take action now. Order all 8 workshop manuals today !

Thank you so much for taking the courses from The Kingdom University. Taking a course is only the first step. We are pleased to present you with the next step—that of going through the process to get rid of all the extra weights that have been slowing and hindering you from fully living out your kingdom assignment.

Call 1 800 558 5020   www.TheKingdomNetwork.org

www.ingramcontent.com/pod-product-compliance
Lightning Source LLC
Chambersburg PA
CBHW040000080526
44586CB00027B/2824